MW00948510

Author: Christy Galatas
Editor: Cody Trahan
Edition: 1st Edition
Published by: Dat Keto Lady LLC.
Publish Date: October 2020
Website: www.datketolady.com

ISBN:9798692447630

©DatKetoLady

To Brett & Ava

Foreword

The words, *"Anyone Can Cook"* (from one of my favorite Disney movies) comes to mind...in this case I'd add the word "KETO" to those words, because this is what Christy always tries to convey...*Anyone Can Cook Keto!*

She wants others to know living the Keto lifestyle doesn't have to be difficult, tasteless or boring...after all, we are from New Orleans where "DELICIOUS FOOD IS LIFE"!

From the beginning, Christy (Dat Keto Lady) has had a heartfelt belief that eating Keto should not only be easy, but sustainable and delicious for the whole family. From cover to cover, **"It's Dinner Time at Our House"** is a reflection of this belief.

Filled with 100 Keto-friendly recipes that contain simple, easy-to-find ingredients, as well as tips and guidance along the way, you'll quickly see how this cookbook expresses Christy's deeply held values about family, faith and Keto sustainability. Throughout, Christy holds to the firm belief that everyone at the dinner table can enjoy Keto meals and **"It's Dinner Time at Our House"** is her way of connecting these beliefs.

Though in the Keto Community you all know Christy as "Dat Keto Lady", I'm thankful to be called her "Mom", and so super proud of who she is as a person... courageous, smart, dedicated, hardworking and a very caring young woman who is fiercely protective of her "circle", which includes all of you in the Keto community.

So happy to be part of her dream becoming a reality...the sky really is the limit!

Now, **"It's Dinner Time at Our House"**

Mom

INTRODUCTION

WELCOME to It's Dinner Time at Our House! My name is Christy Galatas, aka Dat Keto Lady, and I am mom to two beautiful children, author of Big Easy Keto, and a major keto enthusiast based in the New Orleans area. I have lived a ketogenic lifestyle since March 2018, and have taken off almost 50 pounds. Keeping the weight off and maintaining a healthy weight has been the easiest it's ever been because I don't feel deprived of tasty food.

To give you an idea of what my health journey has been like, it took me a year to lose the weight. Remember that this is not a race to the finish line, however, this is a lifelong journey where you will learn so much along the way, and it's ever evolving.

During the weight loss phase of my journey, I did not exercise. I simply changed the foods that I was eating to keto-friendly ones. It wasn't until after I was in my maintenance weight range that I began to incorporate exercise. I also did not include fasting in that time of weight loss. Don't feel pressured to do everything that you read or hear other people doing. There isn't a one-size fits all method. It's your personal journey, and for it to be sustainable, it shouldn't make you miserable. Keep it simple. Find joy in your journey, and watch big things happen.

Whether you're keto, low carb, sugar free, or just enjoy good food, I am thrilled to bring you delicious recipes that everyone at the table will enjoy!

As in my first book, I shared lots of easy recipes that didn't require any special ingredients and were affordable to make. In keeping with the same theme, this book keeps true to that. Living a ketogenic lifestyle shouldn't break the bank and the ingredients should be accessible to everyone without having specialty stores close by.

No matter if you're feeding a large family, or making dinner for one, my hope is that you feel a sense of joy in cooking the recipes in this book. Now let's get cooking!

TABLE OF CONTENTS

NET CARBS & SUGAR ALCOHOLS

How to Calculate Net Carbs:

Each recipe within this book has the Nutritional Information aka "Macros" listed **per serving**.

Here's how to calculate the Net Carbs in each serving:

Carbs - Fiber = Net Carbs

Sugar Alcohols:

Sugar alcohols are sweeteners that look and mostly taste like "regular" sugar, but they don't spike your glucose levels. Thus, they are considered to be keto friendly options when baking and cooking. When reading a Nutrition Facts label, if sugar alcohols are listed, those should be subtracted as well. They may or may not be listed in the Nutrition Facts label.

Keto-friendly sweeteners

Stevia
Erythritol
Monk fruit
Allulose
Xylitol (don't use this one if you have pets in your home)

If sugar alcohols are listed, here's how to calculate Net Carbs:

Carbs - Fiber - Sugar Alcohol = Net Carbs

KETO SWAP OUTS

X Regular Flour ✓ Almond or Coconut Flour

X Milk ✓ Unsweetened nut milk, half & half, heavy whipping cream

X Rice ✓ Riced Cauliflower

X Pasta Noodles ✓ Hearts of Palm Noodles, Spaghetti Squash, Shirataki Noodles

X Sugar ✓ Stevia, Erythritol, Monk Fruit, Allulose

X Potatoes ✓ Radishes, Mashed Cauliflower

X Ice Cream ✓ Sugar Free or Low Carb Ice Cream

X Tortillas ✓ Low Carb Tortillas

X Yogurt ✓ :ratio dairy snack

KETO/LOW-CARB SNACKS

- Cheese (String, Cubed, or Sliced)
- Cheese Wisps
- Black Berries
- Blue Berries
- Strawberries
- Raspberries
- Celery with Perfect Keto Nut Butter
- Pickles
- Olives
- Pepperoni Slices
- Beef Jerky (No Sugar Added)
- Walnuts
- Pork Rinds
- Chia Seed Pudding
- Keto Ice Cream
- :Ratio Dairy Snack
- :Ratio Crunchy Keto Bar
- Almonds
- Brazil Nuts
- Hazelnuts
- Pecans
- Sunflower Seeds
- Avocados
- Cucumbers with ranch dip
- Fat Bombs
- Unsweetened peanut
- butter or nut butter

CAN I DRINK ALCOHOL ON KETO?

The bottom line is yes, but it may impact you differently than others. Drinking alcohol should always be done in moderation and very mindfully. While it may not knock you out of Ketosis, it could potentially stall your weight loss. Below is a list of keto-friendly drinks. Also, keep in mind that liquor that is flavored will often times have added sugars.

- Whiskey
- Vodka
- Tequila
- Rum
- Gin
- Brandy
- Red Wines, these range from 3.4g carbs to 4.5g carbs per serving:
  - Merlot, Pinot Noir, Cabernet, Zinfandel

- White Wines, these range from 1.5 carbs to 5.5g carbs per serving:
  - Sparkling White Wine, Pinot Blanc, Pinot Grigio, Chardonnay, Riesling
- Beer, these range from 1.9g carbs to 3.2g per serving:
  - Budweiser Select 55, Michelob Ultra, Miller Light, Miller 64

- Hard Seltzers, these range from 1g carbs to 4g carbs per serving:
  - White Claw, Truly Spiked, Smirnoff Spiked

You can use liquid drink flavor enhancers like Mio and Crystal Light. Avoid the powdered drink mix-ins because they usually contain Maltodextrin.

HEALTHY OILS & FATS

- Avocado oil
- Avocados
- Butter
- Coconut oil
- Duck fat
- Ghee
- Lard
- Macadamia Nut Oil
- MCT Oil
- Nut Butter
- Olive Oil
- Tallow

PROTEIN

- Beef
- Chicken
- Pork
- Fish
- Bacon
- Deli meat
- Eggs
- Pork rinds
- Sausage
- Wild Game
- Scallops
- Shrimp
- Oysters
- Crawfish

Beans and legumes are NOT low carb or keto-friendly

DAIRY

- Butter
- Cheese, block & shredded
- Cottage Cheese
- Ricotta Cheese
- Cream Cheese
- Eggs
- Sour Cream
- Half & Half
- Unsweetened almond milk
- Heavy Whipping Cream
- Plain Yogurt (unsweetened)
- :ratio dairy snack

Cow's milk, regular yogurt, and low fat or fat free dairy products, and sweetened coffee creamers should be avoided.

SEEDS & NUTS

- Almonds
- Brazil Nuts
- Cashews
- Chia Seeds
- Hazelnuts
- Hemp Seeds
- Macadamia Nuts
- Pecans
- Pistachios
- Sesame Seeds
- Sunflower Seeds
- Walnuts

As with any snacking option, it is important to be mindful of each serving size. Carbs from seeds & nuts can add up rather quickly. I suggest portioning a serving out of the container, instead of eating directly from it.

90 SECOND BREAD

SERVES: 1

PER SERVING

CALORIES: 220

FAT: 21G

PROTEIN: 9G

CARBS: 4G

FIBER: 2G

Ingredients:

- 2 TBS almond flour
- 1 egg
- 1 TBS butter, melted
- 1/8 tsp sweetener (Pyure or similar)
- 1/2 tsp baking powder

Directions:

1. Mix all ingredients in a ramekin or 4 inch square glass dish (I've found these at Target and Marshall's)

2. Microwave on high for 90 seconds.

3. Remove from ramekin

4. slice in half (to make 2 slices of bread).

5. You can also bake this recipe on 375 degrees for 10 minutes in the oven.

6. Toast on each side in a skillet. This is an important step, so don't skip it. It crisps the bread up and makes it so delicious.

90 SECOND GARLIC BREAD

SERVES: 1

PER SERVING

CALORIES: 250

FAT: 22G

PROTEIN: 9G

CARBS: 4G

FIBER: 2G

Ingredients:

- 2 TBS almond flour
- 1 egg
- 1 TBS butter, melted
- 1/8 tsp sweetener (Pyure or similar)
- 1/2 tsp baking powder
- Butter & garlic powder, for topping

Directions:

1. Mix all ingredients in a ramekin or 4 inch square glass dish (I've found these at Target and Marshall's)

2. Microwave on high for 90 seconds.

3. Remove from ramekin

4. slice in half (to make 2 slices of bread).

5. Slather with butter and sprinkle with garlic powder.

6. You can also bake this recipe on 375 degrees for 10 minutes in the oven.

7. Toast on each side in a skillet. This is an important step, so don't skip it. It crisps the bread up and makes it so delicious.

BBQ BRISKET ENDS "MEAT CANDY" PIT BOSS

SERVES: 8

PER SERVING

CALORIES: 420

FAT: 30G

PROTEIN: 35G

CARBS: 2G

FIBER: 0G

Ingredients:

- 5-7 pounds brisket "point"
- 2 tsp kosher salt
- 2 tsp pepper
- 1 tsp cajun seasoning
- 1 1/2 tsp onion powder

- 1 1/2 tsp garlic powder
- 1 cup beef broth
- 1 1/2 cup sugar free bbq sauce
- 3/4 cup golden sweetener (Swerve or Lakanto)

Directions:

1. Preheat smoker/ grill to 225°F

2. Liberally coat all sides of the "point" with seasoning blend.

3. Place the brisket on your smoker/grill, insert thermometer probe, close lid, and smoke until internal temp is 165 degrees (about 5-7 hours)

4. Remove from grill and wrap it snuggly in Pit Boss Butcher Paper.

5. Place back on the smoker/grill, insert thermometer probe, close lid and smoke until internal temp is 190-200 degrees.

6. Remove from smoker/grill, unwrap the meat, and transfer it to an aluminum pan.

7. Cut into cube pieces about 1-2 inches. Toss with BBQ sauce, broth and sweetener

8. Turn the heat up on the smoker/grill to 300 degrees. Place the pan with meat back on the smoker, close the lid and cook for about an hour, stirring every 15 minutes, or so.

9. When the sauce starts to get sticky, and the meat is tender, remove from grill and eat that meat candy!

BBQ CHICKEN SANDWICH

SERVES: 4

PER SERVING

CALORIES: 410

FAT: 27G

PROTEIN: 29G

CARBS: 6G

FIBER: 1G

Ingredients:

- 3 boneless skinless chicken breasts
- 1/4 tsp salt
- 1/4 tsp pepper
- 1/4 tsp garlic powder
- 1/4 tsp onion powder

- 1/2 cup sugar free BBQ sauce
- 2 TBS oil or butter
- 4 Slices of cheddar cheese

90 SECOND BREAD RECIPE (make 4 servings of this for the sandwiches)

Directions:

1. In a skillet, heat oil or butter.

2. Add chicken breasts.

3. Season with salt, pepper, garlic powder, onion powder.

4. USE THE TIME THAT THE CHICKEN IS COOKING TO MAKE THE BREAD FOR EACH SANDWICH. THIS TIMING WILL WORK OUT PERFECTLY BECAUSE THE BREAD WILL BE DONE ABOUT THE SAME TIME THAT THE CHICKEN IS FINISHED.

5. Cook until the chicken is done.

6. Shred the chicken and add bbq sauce.

7. Put bbq chicken mixture on each sandwich and top with a slice of cheese.

BEEF & BROCCOLI

SERVES: 4

PER SERVING

CALORIES: 360

FAT: 25G

PROTEIN: 24G

CARBS: 7G

FIBER: 2G

Ingredients:

Marinade:

- 1/4 cup coconut aminos
- 1 tsp ginger paste
- 3 TBS minced garlic
- 1 tsp sweetener (erythritol or stevia)

Ingredients:

- 1 lb sirloin steak, thinly sliced
- 4 cups broccoli, fresh florets
- 1/4 cup coconut oil
- 1 tsp toasted sesame oil
- 1 tsp soy sauce or coconut aminos
- Sesame seeds

Directions:

1. In a ziploc bag, add marinade and beef. Let this marinate for about 30 minutes.

2. While the beef is marinating, lightly steam broccoli, and drain. You don't want it mushy or too soft. Set aside.

3. Drain marinade off of meat BUT SAVE THIS LIQUID!

4. In a large skillet (I love using my cast iron for this) heat oil and add beef, sesame oil and soy sauce/or coconut aminos.

5. Stir fry beef until it's browned, add broccoli and the remaining marinade that you saved.

6. Top with sesame seeds and serve.

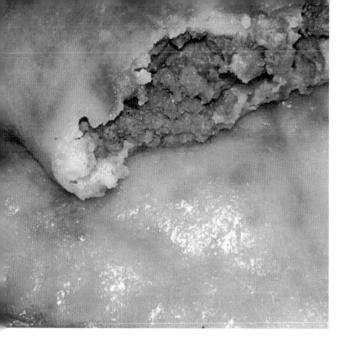

BEEF EMPANADAS

SERVES: 4

PER SERVING

CALORIES: 143

FAT: 10G

PROTEIN: 9G

CARBS: 3G

FIBER: 1G

Ingredients:

DOUGH:

- 1 1/2 cups mozzarella cheese

- 3 oz cream cheese, room temp

- 1 1/4 cup almond flour

- 1 egg

FILLING:

- 1 1/2 lbs ground beef

- 1/2 cup onion, chopped

- 1/2 tsp salt

- 1/2 tsp pepper

- 1/2 TBS chili powder

- 1 tsp cumin

- 1/2 tsp paprika

- Salsa, sour cream (for dipping)

Directions:

1. Preheat oven to 420°F

2. In a pan over medium heat, cook ground beef, and onions, seasoned with salt, pepper, chili powder, cumin and paprika. When it's done, set aside.

3. In a microwave safe bowl, melt mozzarella cheese and cream cheese, in 30 second increments. Stirring in between.

4. Add almond flour and egg and blend well.

5. Separate dough into 8 balls and flatten each one into a circular shape.

6. Fill each circle with meat mixture and fold dough over. Press and seal each seam.

7. Place on baking sheet and put in oven

8. Bake for 12 minutes, or until dough is golden on top.

BEEF STROGANOFF

SERVES: 4

PER SERVING

CALORIES: 495

FAT: 20G

PROTEIN: 40G

CARBS: 3G

FIBER: 1G

Ingredients:

- 1 pound ground beef
- 1 1/2 cups beef broth or stock
- 1 cup mushrooms, sliced
- 1/4 cup onions, chopped
- 2 TBS minced garlic
- 1/2 tsp salt
- 1 tsp pepper
- 1/4 tsp Cajun seasoning
- 1/2 cup heavy whipping cream
- 1/2-1 tsp xanthan or guar gum
- 2 packs pasta substitute (Natural Heaven, Pasta Zero, or Zoodles)

Directions:

1. In a large skillet, add ground beef, salt, pepper, onions, mushrooms, garlic, and Cajun seasoning.

2. When the meat is done and onions are tender, lower heat and add broth, cream and xanthan gum. You'll have to whisk this well to dissolve the thickener (xanthan or guar gum) and make a nice gravy.

3. Remove from heat and serve over pasta substitute.

BEEF TIPS AND GRAVY

SERVES: 6

PER SERVING

CALORIES: 455

FAT: 30G

PROTEIN: 46G

CARBS: 4G

FIBER: 0G

Ingredients:

- 2 lbs chuck roast, cubed
- 2 TBS avocado oil
- 1 tsp salt
- 1/2 tsp cajun seasoning
- 1 tsp pepper
- 1/2 tsp garlic powder
- 1/2 cup onion, chopped
- 3 cups beef broth
- 1 TBS sweetener
- 2 TBS tomato paste
- 2 TBS Worcestershire sauce
- 1/4 tsp xanthan or guar gum

Directions:

1. In a pot, over medium high heat, add oil, meat, salt, cajun seasoning, pepper, garlic powder, and onion. Cook until the meat is just beginning to soften and the meat is seared on all sides. Remove from the skillet, and set aside.

2. Reduce the heat, and in the same pot, add the remaining ingredients.

3. Simmer for about 5 minutes and dissolve the xanthan gum completely.

4. Reduce heat to low and add meat back into skillet with gravy and stir well.

5. Cover with lid, and cook for 20-30 minutes.

BLUE CHEESE DRESSING

SERVES: 2 TBS

PER SERVING

CALORIES: 105

FAT: 12G

PROTEIN: 1G

CARBS: 1G

FIBER: 0G

Ingredients:

- 1 cup mayonnaise

- 1/2 cup sour cream

- 1/2 TBS lemon juice

- 1 tsp Worcestershire sauce

- 1/2 tsp garlic powder

- 1/4 tsp salt

- 1/2 tsp black pepper

- 1/2 cup blue cheese crumbles

Directions:

1. Put all ingredients in a bowl and mix until well combined.

2. Refrigerate for at least an hour prior to serving.

3. Store in an airtight container.

BREADED PORK CHOPS

SERVES: 6

PER SERVING

CALORIES: 348

FAT: 21G

PROTEIN: 37G

CARBS: 1G

FIBER: 0G

Ingredients:

- 1 pork loin (cut this into 1" thick pork chops) 6 chops total
- 1/4 cup avocado oil

BREADING INGREDIENTS

- 1/2 cup Parmesan cheese
- 1 cup crushed pork rinds
- 1/2 tsp onion powder
- 1/2 tsp garlic powder
- 1 tsp Italian seasoning
- 1/2 tsp pepper
- 1/4 tsp Cajun seasoning

Directions:

1. Lay pork loin out and cut chops.

2. In a mixing bowl, combine all "BREADING INGREDIENTS".

3. Coat each side of the pork chops in breading and set aside.

4. In a large skillet, heat oil.

5. Carefully place each chop into the oil, and cook on each side for approximately 3 minutes per side.

6. Remove from skillet, and place on a rack to drain excess oil. This step will ensure that your pork chops aren't soggy.

BRISKET WITH PIT BOSS

SERVES: 20

PER SERVING

CALORIES: 330

FAT: 10G

PROTEIN: 36G

CARBS: 0G

FIBER: 0G

Ingredients:

My preferred method to cook a brisket is to smoke it on my PitBoss KC Combo (linked below)

- 12-15 lb brisket, trimmed

- 2 TBS Kosher salt

- 2 TBS pepper

- 2 TBS garlic powder

- 2 TBS onion powder

- Sugar free bbq sauce (optional topping)

Directions:

1. Preheat smoker to 225°F

2. In a mixing bowl, combine all of your seasonings well.

3. Liberally coat all sides of the brisket with seasoning blend.

4. Place brisket on the grill/smoker, and insert thermometer probe. Close the lid, and smoke the brisket until internal temperature is 165 degrees (around 7 hours)

5. Remove brisket from the grill/ smoker.

6. At this point you can separate the "flat" from the "point" or you can leave it as one whole piece.

7. Fully wrap the meat in Pit Boss Butcher paper.

8. Return the brisket to the grill/ smoker. Reinsert thermometer probe, close the lid, and keep the temp at 225 degrees. (around 5-6 hours)

9. When the internal temp reaches 190-200 in the thickest part of the meat, take it off of the grill.

10. Do not unwrap the meat. Allow it to rest for at least an hour before slicing it. I put it in a cooler or in the over (turned off, of course) just to let it rest.

11. Remove the paper from the brisket, slice and serve.

BUFFALO STUFFED CHICKEN

SERVES: 4

PER SERVING

CALORIES: 412

FAT: 15G

PROTEIN: 40G

CARBS: 5G

FIBER: 0G

Ingredients:

- 4 boneless skinless chicken breasts, make a butterfly cut in them (for stuffing)

- Salt & pepper, to taste

- 1/8 tsp cajun seasoning

- 4 oz cream cheese, room temp

- 1/4 cup bacon, cooked & crumbled

- 1/2 cup shredded cheddar cheese

- 1/4 cup Moore's creamy buffalo ranch sauce

- 3 TBS ranch salad dressing

- Toppings: buffalo sauce, ranch, parsley

Directions:

1. Preheat oven to 350°F

2. Sprinkle each chicken breast with salt, pepper, and cajun seasoning. Place in 9x13 baking dish.

3. In a mixing bowl, combine cream cheese, bacon shredded cheese buffalo sauce and ranch.

4. Spoon filling that you just made into the cavity/pocket of each chicken breast and spoon just a bit of buffalo sauce on top of each breast after you've filled it.

5. Place in oven and bake for 22-25 minutes.

6. Remove from oven when fully cooked, and drizzle with buffalo sauce, ranch and sprinkle with parsley.

BURRITO BOWL

SERVES: 4

PER SERVING

CALORIES: 143

FAT: 10G

PROTEIN: 9G

CARBS: 3G

FIBER: 1G

Ingredients:

- 2 lbs ground beef
- 1/2 tsp salt
- 1/2 tsp pepper
- 1/4 tsp onion powder
- 1/4 tsp garlic powder
- 1 TBS chili powder

- 1 tsp cumin
- 1 tsp paprika
- See Faux Refried Beans recipe
- See Sour cream drizzle
- Lettuce, tomato, avocado or guacamole, cilantro, shredded cheese, black olives.

Directions:

1. In a skillet, cook ground beef with salt, pepper, onion powder, garlic powder, chili powder, cumin and paprika. Set aside.

2. Make Faux Refried Beans, and set aside.

3. In each bowl, layer meat, beans, cheese, and all toppings. Finish with sour cream drizzle.

BUTTERY GARLIC MASHED "TATERS"

SERVES: 6

PER SERVING

CALORIES: 90

FAT: 10G

PROTEIN: 2G

CARBS: 3G

FIBER: 1G

Ingredients:

- 2 (10 oz) bags, frozen riced cauliflower
- 8 TBS butter, room temp
- 1 TBS minced garlic
- 3 oz cream cheese, room temp, cubed
- 1/2 tsp salt
- 1/2 tsp cajun seasoning
- 1 tsp pepper
- 1/2 TBS parsley

Directions:

1. Steam and drain riced cauliflower according to the directions on the package.

2. In a mixing bowl, add all of the ingredients and combine them well.

3. Using an immersion blender, completely blend it all to a smooth consistency. If you don't have and immersion blender, a food processor, or stand blender would work well, too.

BUTTERY GARLIC STEAK BITES

SERVES: 4

PER SERVING

CALORIES: 320

FAT: 19G

PROTEIN: 37G

CARBS: 1G

FIBER: 0G

Ingredients:

- 1 1/2 lbs sirloin, cubed
- 4 TBS butter
- 1/2 tsp salt
- 1/2 tsp pepper

- 1/2 tsp onion powder
- 1/4 tsp Cajun seasoning
- 3 TBS soy sauce
- 3 TBS minced garlic

Directions:

1. In a bowl, combine meat, salt, pepper, Cajun seasoning, soy sauce, onion powder and garlic.

2. Let it marinate for 15-20 minutes.

3. In a skillet, on high heat, (I like using cast iron for this one) add butter.

4. Remove steak bites in batches from marinade, leave excess liquid out, and add to skillet.

5. You don't want to pile them on top of each other. Make a single layer at a time.

6. Cook steak bites for 3-4 minutes, stirring occasionally until they are golden brown.

7. Repeat as necessary until all pieces are cooked.

BUTTERY ITALIAN SHRIMP

SERVES: 4

PER SERVING

CALORIES: 435

FAT: 35G

PROTEIN: 29G

CARBS: 5G

FIBER: 1G

Ingredients:

- 2 TBS avocado oil
- 5 TBS butter
- 2 lbs shrimp, thawed & shells removed
- 1/2 tsp salt
- 1/2 tsp pepper
- 1/2 tsp onion powder
- 1/4 tsp cajun seasoning

- 3 TBS minced garlic
- 1 cup cherry tomatoes, halved
- 3 cups spinach, fresh
- 3/4 cup heavy whipping cream
- 1/4 cup Parmesan cheese
- 2 TBS parsley

Directions:

1. In a skillet, heat oil and butter over medium high heat.

2. Add shrimp, salt, pepper, onion powder, cajun seasoning, and garlic.

3. Sauté the shrimp until the just start to turn pink.

4. Reduce heat to simmer and add cream, tomatoes, spinach, Parmesan cheese and parsley.

5. Stir until the sauce is nice and creamy. Remove from heat. The sauce will thicken.

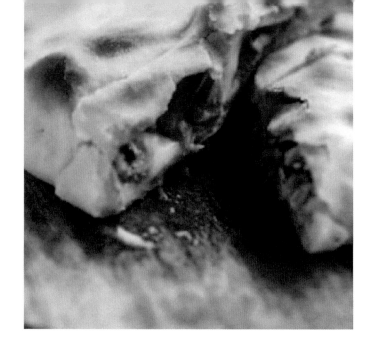

CALZONES

SERVES: 6

PER SERVING

CALORIES: 620

FAT: 38G

PROTEIN: 29G

CARBS: 9G

FIBER: 2G

Ingredients:

DOUGH INGREDIENTS

- 3 cups mozzarella cheese

- 1 1/2 cups almond flour

- 4 oz cream cheese, room temp

- 2 egg

- 1 TBS active dry yeast

- 1 TBS baking powder

- 1 TBS sweetener

- 1/2 tsp garlic powder

- 1 tsp Italian seasoning

FILLING INGREDIENTS

1/2 cup pizza sauce

1 1/4 cup mozzarella cheese

Pepperoni slices 2 TBS parsley

Directions:

1. Preheat oven to 400°F

2. In a microwave safe bowl, add mozzarella cheese and cream cheese.

3. Microwave in 30 increments, stirring between

4. When it's melted, add almond flour, yeast, baking powder, sweetener, egg, garlic powder & Italian seasoning

5. Mix to combine well

6. Divide into 6 equal dough balls

7. Roll each ball out into circular shapes between parchment paper

8. Spoon pizza sauce into the center of each circle, and add cheese and pepperoni.

9. Fold each circle over to make a half-moon shape, and press opening together to seal

10. Bake in oven for 15-20 minutes, or until it's slightly golden on top

CARNE ASADA POBLANO PEPPERS

SERVES: 4

PER SERVING

CALORIES: 387

FAT: 25G

PROTEIN: 33G

CARBS: 6G

FIBER: 1G

Ingredients:

- 2 lb beef roast, rump or chuck, cubed small
- 4 TBS minced garlic
- 1 jalapeño pepper (seeded & minced)
- 2 tsp cumin
- 3 TBS cilantro, chopped
- 2 TBS apple cider vinegar
- 1 tsp sweetener
- 1/2 cup avocado oil
- Juice of 2 limes
- Coat meat in salt & pepper
- 4 - 6 poblano peppers (depending on size)

SEE CHEESE SAUCE RECIPE

Directions:

1. Preheat oven to 350°F

2. Wash peppers, remove tops, de seed them and slice in half lengthwise

3. In a skillet on high heat, cook meat until meat is almost done, but not quite. Remove from heat.

4. Make cheese sauce.

5. In a 9x13 baking dish, lay peppers out and spoon the beef mixture into each one.

6. Top meat and peppers with cheese sauce.

7. Cover the baking dish with aluminum foil.

8. Bake for approximately 25 minutes.

9. Remove foil and bake for an additional 5 minutes uncovered.

CAULI
MAC & CHEESE

SERVES: 6

PER SERVING

CALORIES: 218

FAT: 16G

PROTEIN: 9G

CARBS: 6G

FIBER: 2G

Ingredients:

- 2 (12 oz) bags frozen cauliflower
- 2 oz full fat cream cheese, room temp
- 1/4 cup heavy whipping cream
- 1 1/2 cups cheddar cheese, shredded
- 1/4 tsp salt
- 1/2 tsp pepper
- 1 tsp pepper
- 1/4 tsp Cajun seasoning
- Bacon, optional mix-in

Directions:

- Steam cauliflower according to instructions on package, drain and chop into small pieces.

Microwave method:

1. Add chopped cauliflower to microwave safe bowl, and add all remaining ingredients.

2. Mix it up and microwave for 3 minutes.

3. Remove from microwave and stir it up to combine it all well.

4. If the cheese needs to be melted more, microwave for an additional 1-2 minutes.

Stovetop method:

1. Add chopped cauliflower to pot, over medium to low heat.

2. Add all other ingredients, and stir to combine and to melt cheese fully.

3. This will take approximately 3-5 minutes.

CHAFFLE
(CHEESY WAFFLE)

SERVES: 1 (2 CHAFFLES)

PER SERVING

CALORIES: 202

FAT: 13G

PROTEIN: 16G

CARBS: 0G

FIBER: 0G

Ingredients:

- 1 large egg

- 1/2 cup shredded cheese (cheddar, mozzarella, or your favorite)

- Sprinkle of salt

- Favorite seasonings, to taste

Directions:

1. Preheat waffle maker

2. In a bowl, whisk together all of your ingredients

3. Spray waffle maker with nonstick spray, and pour in half of mixture and cook for 2-3 minutes. Remove and add remaining mixture.

4. If you want to make this a sweet recipe, add sweetener, cinnamon, cocoa powder, etc and top with sugar free syrup. This is a super versatile recipe that can be modified in so many ways.

CHEESE SAUCE

SERVES: 6

PER 3 TBS SERVING

CALORIES: 130

FAT: 5G

PROTEIN: 1G

CARBS: 0G

FIBER: 0G

Ingredients:

- 8 oz cheese, shredded YOUR FAVORITE KIND
- 1 cup heavy whipping cream
- 4 TBS butter
- 1/8-1/4 cup water

Directions:

1. Combine all ingredients in a saucepan and cook over low heat.

2. Stir often, until everything is melted and well combined.

3. Remove from heat.

CHEESE SHELL TACOS

SERVES: 4

PER SERVING

CALORIES: 432

FAT: 33G

PROTEIN: 28G

CARBS: 4G

FIBER: 2G

Ingredients:

Meat

- 1 pound ground beef
- 1 1/2 TBS chili powder
- 1 tsp cumin
- 1 tsp paprika
- 1/2 tsp onion powder
- 1/2 tsp salt
- 1/2 tsp pepper

Cheese Shells

- 9 oz. shredded cheddar cheese
- Parchment Paper

Toppings

- Lettuce
- Tomato
- Sour Cream
- Avocado

Directions:

1. Brown ground beef in skillet with seasonings

2. While the meat is cooking, make cheese shells

3. Spread a circle (about 1/4 cup) of shredded cheese on parchment paper and microwave for 90 seconds

4. Immediately remove from microwave and stand cooked circle of cheese between to objects (like cans or cups) to make shell take on its taco shape

5. The cheese should be the color of a Dorito (lol)

6. Stuff shells with meat and toppings

CHEESE STUFFED MEATBALLS & MARINARA

SERVES: 6 (24 MEATBALLS)

PER SERVING

CALORIES: 440

FAT: 23G

PROTEIN: 20G

CARBS: 3G

FIBER: 0G

Ingredients:

- 1 lb ground beef
- 1 lb ground sausage
- 1 TBS Italian seasoning
- 1/2 tsp salt
- 1 tsp pepper
- 1 TBS parsley
- 1/2 tsp garlic powder
- 1/2 tsp onion powder

- 1/4 cup Parmesan cheese
- 12 oz mozzarella, cubed (you could even use string cheese cut up for this)
- 16 oz. marinara/pasta sauce NO SUGAR ADDED (read the ingredient list on the label)

Directions:

1. Preheat oven to 400°F

2. In a large bowl, combine all of the ingredients EXCEPT for the pasta sauce.

3. Take golf ball sized piece of meat mixture and place a cube of cheese in the middle, then form a meatball. Make sure you seal the meat all the way around the cheese.

4. Bake in the oven for 15-18 minutes, or until meat is fully cooked.

5. In a saucepan, heat marinara.

6. When the meatballs are cooked, serve with a side of sauce for dipping.

CHEESY FLUFFY EGGS

SERVES: 4

PER SERVING

CALORIES: 455

FAT: 39G

PROTEIN: 25G

CARBS: 1G

FIBER: 0G

Ingredients:

- 8 eggs

- 2 cups shredded cheese, your favorite kind

- 5 TBS butter

- Salt, pepper, & parsley, to taste

Directions:

1. In a mixing bowl, vigorously whisk eggs, cheese and seasonings.

2. In a skillet, over medium low heat, melt butter

3. Pour egg & cheese mixture into skillet and begin stirring with spatula.

4. Keep eggs from sticking to the pan by scraping the sides and bottom.

5. The key to the perfect eggs is you want them to be a light yellow color...NO brown parts.

6. As soon as there are no more liquid parts of the eggs, they are done.

7. Remove from skillet and serve.

CHICKEN & CHAFFLE

SERVES: 4

PER SERVING

CALORIES: 597

FAT: 38G

PROTEIN: 54G

CARBS: 2G

FIBER: 0G

Ingredients:

Chicken

- 3 chicken breasts, sliced into tenders
- 1/2 cup Parmesan cheese
- 1 cup crushed pork rinds
- 1/2 tsp onion powder
- 1/2 tsp garlic powder
- 1 tsp Italian seasoning
- 1/2 tsp pepper
- 1/4 tsp Cajun seasoning
- 1/2 cup avocado oil

Chaffle

- 3 large eggs
- 1 1/2 cups shredded cheese (cheddar or mozzarella)
- Sprinkle of salt

- 1/8 tsp garlic powder

Queso

- 1/4 cup heavy whipping cream
- 1 oz cream cheese, room temp
- 1/4 cup shredded cheese (your favorite kind)

Directions:

Chicken

1. In a bowl, make your breading by mixing parmesan cheese, pork rinds, onion powder, garlic powder, Italian seasoning, pepper and Cajun seasoning.

2. Coat the chicken in this breading mixture.

3. In a skillet, heat oil and cook chicken tenders that you've breaded.

Chaffle

4. Preheat waffle maker

5. In a bowl, mix all of the "CHAFFLE INGREDIENTS"

6. Spray waffle maker with nonstick spray, and pour in half of mixture

7. Cook for 2-3 minutes.

8. Remove and add remaining mixture.

9. This should make 4 Chaffles

Queso

10. Make queso last.

11. In a measuring cup, add all "Queso Ingredients" in a measuring cup or microwave safe bowl.

12. Microwave in 30 second increments, stirring in between each segment, until it's melted well.

CHICKEN & SAUSAGE GUMBO

SERVES: 8

PER SERVING

CALORIES: 375

FAT: 30G

PROTEIN: 29G

CARBS: 4G

FIBER: 1G

Ingredients:

ROUX

- 1 cup chopped onion
- 1/2 cup chopped celery
- 1/2 cup chopped green bell pepper
- 8 tablespoons salted butter or oil
- 1 1/2 cup chicken broth, or seafood stock
- 1/2 teaspoon salt
- 1/2 tsp. Xanthan gum

Gumbo

- 1 whole chicken (3-4 lbs) OR boneless skinless chicken thighs OR boneless skinless chicken breast (cooked & shredded) I PREFER TO USE THIGHS, BUT A TIMESAVING TIP WOULD BE TO USE A ROTISSERIE CHICKEN
- 1 (14 oz) pack smoked sausage, chopped
- 6 cups chicken stock or broth

- 1 bay leaf
- 2 tsp cajun seasoning
- 1 tsp salt
- 2 tsp pepper
- 3 TBS minced garlic
- 1 TBS parsley
- 2 cups okra, chopped, optional (I prefer using frozen)
- Serve over cauliflower rice that you've steamed, drained, and seasoned with salt & butter

Directions:

In a cast iron skillet, over medium high heat, put butter, salt and veggies.

Stir for about 10 minutes, when the veggies start to brown, start to stir more frequently to make sure that it does not stick to the bottom of the skillet and burn.

In a measuring cup, heat up broth (approx. 3 mins), then whisk in the xanthan gum. Whisk until dissolved. This combination is what will give your gumbo a thickness (instead of adding flour.)

4. Add the mixture to the skillet of caramelized veggies, stir well. Turn off heat.

5. Transfer your "Roux" into a large stockpot. Next, pour in chicken broth.

6. Add all of your seasonings and okra.

7. Bring this to a boil; reduce heat, and simmer for 35 minutes.

8. Add chicken and sausage. Cook for 10-15 minutes until it's heated throughout.

CHICKEN CARBONAR

SERVES: 6

PER SERVING

CALORIES: 410

FAT: 14G

PROTEIN: 35G

CARBS: 4G

FIBER: 1G

Ingredients:

- 2 lbs boneless skinless chicken thighs, cut into cubes
- 5 slices bacon, cooked & crumbled
- 1/2 cup onion, chopped
- 1/2 tsp salt
- 1/2 tsp pepper
- 1/2 tsp cajun seasoning
- 1 tsp Italian seasoning
- 2 TBS avocado oil or butter
- 1 TBS minced garlic
- 1 cup heavy whipping cream
- 1 cup chicken broth
- 1/3 cup Parmesan cheese
- 2 cups fresh spinach
- Pasta substitute, Pasta Zero, Natural Heaven, Zoodles or spaghetti squash

Directions:

1. In a skillet over medium heat, add oil and cook chicken with salt, pepper, Cajun seasoning, and Italian seasoning.

2. Once the chicken is cooked, remove from skillet, and lower the heat.

3. To the skillet, add onions and spinach. Sauté them until they are tender.

4. Add minced garlic, heavy whipping cream, broth, and Parmesan cheese.

5. Simmer the sauce, but DO NOT boil, for about 5 minutes.

6. Add chicken and bacon to the sauce in the skillet, and mix well to coat chicken with sauce.

7. Serve over pasta substitute

CHICKEN CORDON BLEU

SERVES: 6

PER SERVING

CALORIES: 455

FAT: 35G

PROTEIN: 32G

CARBS: 4G

FIBER: 1G

Ingredients:

- 4 cups chicken, shredded (rotisserie chicken works great in this recipe)
- 8 oz ham, deli style, cubed
- 4 TBS butter, melted
- 6 oz cream cheese, room temp & cubed
- 1 TBS Dijon mustard
- 6 slices provolone cheese
- 1/2 cup cheddar cheese, shredded
- 1/4 tsp salt

- 1/2 tsp pepper
- 1/4 tsp cajun seasoning
- 1/4 tsp onion powder
- 1/4 tsp garlic powder

Directions:

1. Preheat oven to 350°F
2. In a large mixing bowl, combine all ingredients **EXCEPT FOR PROVOLONE CHEESE** and stir until well combined
3. Transfer mixture into a 9 inch baking dish.
4. Top with sliced provolone cheese
5. Bake for 25 minutes, or until cheese is melted and bubbly on top. If you want it a bit golden on top, broil it for a minute or two.

CHICKEN ÉTOUFFÉE

SERVES: 6

PER SERVING

CALORIES: 375

FAT: 19G

PROTEIN: 22G

CARBS: 4G

FIBER: 1G

Ingredients:

- 1 cup chopped onion
- 1/2 cup chopped celery
- 1/2 cup chopped green bell pepper
- 8 tablespoons salted butter or oil
- 1 1/2 cup chicken broth
- 1/2 teaspoon salt
- 1/2 tsp Cajun seasoning
- 1/2 tsp pepper
- 1/4 tsp onion powder
- 1/4 tsp garlic powder
- 1/2 tsp. Xanthan gum
- 3 chicken breasts (cooked & shredded), or a rotisserie chicken
- 1 bag frozen riced cauliflower, cooked according to the directions on pkg

Directions:

1. In a large pot, heat butter OR oil and add chicken, onion, celery, bell pepper, salt, Cajun seasoning, pepper, onion powder, and garlic powder.

2. Cook this down until the chopped seasonings are tender and chicken is done.

3. Remove chicken and shred it up.

4. Add broth and xanthan gum, whisk well to dissolve and thicken.

5. Add chicken back into pot and simmer for approximately 10 minutes.

6. Serve over cauliflower rice.

CHICKEN FAJITA SOUP

SERVES: 8

PER SERVING

CALORIES: 201

FAT: 10G

PROTEIN: 26G

CARBS: 7G

FIBER: 2G

Ingredients:

- 2 lbs boneless skinless chicken breast, cubed OR rotisserie chicken
- 4 TBS avocado oil OR butter
- 1/2 cup onion, chopped
- 1/2 cup green bell pepper, chopped
- 1/2 cup yellow bell pepper, chopped
- 2 TBS minced garlic
- 1 tsp salt
- 1 tsp pepper
- 2 tsp cumin
- 1 TBS chili powder
- 2 tsp paprika
- 2 (10 oz) cans dices tomatoes (like Rotel)
- 3 cups chicken broth
- 1 cup fiesta blend cheese, for topping

Directions:

1. In a pot, heat oil. Add chicken, onions, bell peppers, garlic, salt, pepper, cumin, chili powder, and paprika.

2. When the chicken is cooked, reduce the head and add the remaining ingredients to the pot.

3. Cook on low until the soup is heated throughout.

OPTIONAL COOKING METHOD:

Slow cooker: Add all ingredients to slow cooker and cook on low for 8 hours or on high for 4 hours.

Instant Pot: Add all ingredients to the Instant Pot and set manual time to 30 minutes, or use the "Soup" setting.

CHICKEN PARMESAN

SERVES: 6

PER SERVING

CALORIES: 442

FAT: 17G

PROTEIN: 31G

CARBS: 6G

FIBER: 1G

Ingredients:

- 2 pounds chicken breast
- 1 cup crushed pork rinds
- 1/4 cup grated Parmesan cheese
- 1/2 tsp garlic powder
- 1/2 tsp onion powder
- 1 tsp Italian seasoning
- 1 tsp parsley
- 1 jar sugar free/no sugar added marinara sauce
- 1 cup mozzarella cheese

Directions:

1. Preheat oven to 350°F

2. In a bowl make the "breading" by combining crushed pork rinds, Parmesan cheese, garlic powder, onion powder, Italian seasoning, and parsley.

3. If the chicken breasts are really thick, I recommend slicing them in half (butterfly cut).

4. Coat them in the breading mixture and place them in a baking dish (9x13).

5. Top with the marinara sauce and mozzarella cheese.

6. Bake for 30 minutes.

CHICKEN POT PIE

SERVES: 8

PER SERVING

CALORIES: 225

FAT: 12G

PROTEIN: 24G

CARBS: 7G

FIBER: 3G

Ingredients:

Filling Ingredients:

- 3 TBS avocado oil OR butter
- 1 1/2 lb chicken breast, cooked & shredded, (a rotisserie chicken works great)
- 1/4 cup onion, finely chopped
- 1/2 cup celery, finely chopped
- 1 1/4 cups peas & carrots, frozen

- 1 TBS minced garlic
- 1/2 tsp salt
- 1 tsp pepper
- 1 TBS parsley
- 3/4 cup chicken broth
- 1/4 cup peas, frozen
- 1/2 cup heavy whipping cream
- 4 oz cream cheese, room temp

Topping Ingredients:

- 1 cup almond flour
- 1 TBS coconut flour
- 1 1/2 tsp baking powder
- 2 TBS butter, room temp
- 2 TBS sour cream
- 1/2 TBS sweetener
- 1/4 tsp garlic powder
- 1 egg
- 2 TBS butter, melted to brush top of crust

Directions:

1. Preheat oven to 400°F
2. Grease 9" pie pan or baking dish
3. In a large skillet, over medium heat, add oil, onions, and celery. Cook for a few minutes until they are tender. Remove from heat
4. In a mixing bowl, add the remaining "Filling" ingredients and combine well.
5. Transfer "Filling" to baking dish.
6. In a mixing bowl, combine all of "Topping" ingredients. Blend until it is well combined and smooth
7. Place the dough between two pieces of parchment paper, and roll into a flat (9ish inch circle)
8. Lay dough on top of filling.
9. Bake for 10-12 minutes, or until crust is golden on top.
10. Let the pie rest for 5 or so minutes before serving.

CHICKEN SPAGHETTI

SERVES: 12

PER SERVING

CALORIES: 346

FAT: 21G

PROTEIN: 15G

CARBS: 8G

FIBER: 1G

Ingredients:

- 3 cups chicken breast, cooked & shredded (Rotisserie chicken/pre-cooked, or even canned chicken works just fine)

- 2 (10 oz) cans Rotel

- 16 oz full fat cream cheese, room temp

- 2 cups sour cream

- 2 cups sharp cheddar cheese, shredded

- 1 tsp salt

- 1 tsp pepper

- 2 tsp parsley

- 1/2 cup half & half

- 1 stick butter (salted)

- 1/2 tsp Cajun seasoning (like Tony's)

- 1 cup sharp cheddar cheese (for topping) don't melt this (SET ASIDE)

- 2 1/2 cups OR 2 packs Pasta substitute (I LOVE Natural Heaven angel hair, which is made of hearts of palm) spaghetti squash would work, or Pasta Zero

Directions:

1. Preheat oven to 350°F

2. In a large bowl, combine and melt everything in the microwave (EXCEPT chicken and pasta)

3. In a baking dish (9x13) lay out pasta substitute. Pour melted cheese & cream mixture, and add chicken, them mix it all up.

4. Top with the 1 cup shredded cheddar.

5. Bake for approximately 12 minutes, or until cheese is melted on top.

6. Makes 12 servings (Because you're gonna want these LEFTOVERS!)

CHICKEN TENDERS

SERVES: 4

PER SERVING

CALORIES: 310

FAT: 15G

PROTEIN: 33G

CARBS: 2G

FIBER: 0G

Ingredients:

- 3 boneless skinless chicken breasts, cut into tenders

- 1 egg

- 1/2 cup heavy whipping cream

- 1 cup pork rinds, crushed

- 1/4 cup Parmesan cheese

- 1/2 tsp salt

- 1 tsp pepper

- 1/2 tsp cajun seasoning

- 1/4 tsp onion powder

- 1/4 tsp garlic powder

- 1 tsp parsley

- Oil (optional if deep frying, and not using air fryer)

- Moores Creamy Buffalo Ranch sauce

Directions:

1. In a mixing bowl, add egg, and heavy whipping cream and beat with a fork

2. In another bowl, add pork rinds, Parmesan cheese, and powdered seasonings

3. Dip each tender into liquid mixture first, then dredge in pork rind "crunchy" batter. Continue until all tenders have been coated.

4. Lay them flat in air fryer

5. Cook on 350 degrees for 12 minutes, or until center of chicken is done.

6. Toss tenders in sauce & serve

OPTIONAL COOKING METHOD

Prepare the same way, but don't use air fryer. In a pan, heat oil and cook on each side for 5 minutes on each side. Remove from oil, and set on a rack to drain.

CHICKEN WINGS

SERVES: 4

PER SERVING

CALORIES: 330

FAT: 14G

PROTEIN: 26G

CARBS: 0G

FIBER: 0G

Ingredients:

- 2 pounds chicken wings
- 1/2 - 1 TBS Cajun seasoning
- Parmesan cheese
- Buffalo sauce
- Ranch dip (optional)

Directions:

1. Preheat oven to 420°F
2. Line pan with parchment paper (for easy cleanup)
3. Lay wings flat on pan (no seasoning on them, they're naked while baking)
4. Bake for one hour. Remove from oven, and place wings in a bowl. Coat with seasoning and parmesan cheese and serve.

CHILE RELLENO SOUP

SERVES: 6

PER SERVING

CALORIES: 562

FAT: 39G

PROTEIN: 41G

CARBS: 5G

FIBER: 1G

Ingredients:

- 5 poblano peppers, stems & seeds removed, chopped into about 1 inch squares

- 1 lb boneless skinless chicken breasts, cubed

- 4 TBS avocado oil

- 1/4 cup onion

- 3 TBS minced garlic

- 1 tsp cumin

- 1 tsp paprika

- 1/2 TBS chili powder

- 1/2 tsp salt

- 1/2 tsp pepper

- 4 cup chicken stock or broth

- 8 oz full fat cream cheese, cubed

- 2 cups Fiesta blend cheese, shredded

- 1 cup cheddar cheese, shredded (for topping)

Directions:

1. In a large pot, over medium heat, add oil and cook peppers, chicken, onions & garlic.

2. Season with salt, pepper, cumin, paprika and chili powder.

3. When the meat is cooked, and peppers are tender, add broth, cream cheese, and fiesta blend cheese.

4. Stir until cheeses are melted and soup is heated throughout.

5. Serve and top each bowl of soup with cheddar cheese

OPTIONAL COOKING METHOD:

Slow cooker: Add all of the ingredients to slow cooker. Cook on low for 8 hours, or high for 4 hours.

Instant Pot: Add all of the ingredients to the Instant Pot, cook on manual time setting for 25 minutes

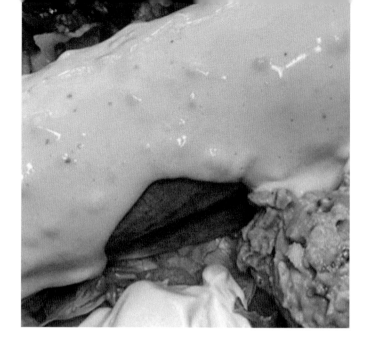

CHIMICHANGAS

SERVES: 4

PER SERVING

CALORIES: 445

FAT: 30G

PROTEIN: 24G

CARBS: 10G

FIBER: 5G

Ingredients:

- 4 low carb tortillas

- 1 lb ground beef OR shredded chicken

- 1 TBS chili powder

- 1 tsp cumin

- 1 tsp paprika

- 1/2 tsp salt

- 1/2 tsp pepper

- 1/4 tsp onion powder

- 1/4 tsp garlic powder

- 1 cup Mexican blend, shredded cheese

- 4 TBS enchilada sauce

- Optional toppings, guacamole, lettuce, tomato, olives, salsa, sour cream

- SEE CHEESE SAUCE RECIPE

Directions:

1. Preheat oven to 375°F

2. In a skillet, cook ground beef with all of the powdered seasonings listed. Remove from heat.

3. Lay out tortillas and spoon equal amounts of beef into each one. Add shredded cheese and enchilada sauce roll tortillas up.

4. Transfer to a baking dish.

5. Bake for 5-10 minutes, or until tortillas are crispy.

6. Remove from oven, plate them up, and top with "Cheese Sauce"

OPTIONAL COOKING METHODS:

Air Fryer: 375 degrees for 5-10 minutes

Stovetop: Deep fry in oil of your choice until tortillas are golden.

CHUNKY STEW OVER "RICE"

SERVES: 6

PER SERVING

CALORIES: 412

FAT: 24G

PROTEIN: 37G

CARBS: 11G

FIBER: 3G

Ingredients:

- 2 lb tender chuck roast, cubed into 1 inch pieces
- 1/2 tsp salt
- 1/2 tsp pepper
- 1/2 tsp cajun seasoning
- 3 TBS avocado oil
- 1/2 cup onion, chopped
- 1 1/2 cup carrots, frozen
- 2 TBS minced garlic

- 1 tsp Italian seasoning
- 1 TBS parsley
- 1/2 cup celery, chopped
- 1/2 cup peas, frozen
- 1 cup radishes, cut into quarters
- 6 cups beef broth or stock
- 1 14.5 oz can diced tomatoes
- 1 (10 oz) bag riced cauliflower, steamed & drained (this is what you will serve the stew over

Directions:

1. In a large pot, over medium heat, add meat, salt, pepper, cajun seasoning, onion, Italian seasoning, parsley, celery and radishes.

2. Cook until meat is done and chopped seasonings are tender and beginning to caramelize on the bottom of pot.

3. Deglaze the pot by pouring in the broth and scraping the bottom of the pots.

4. Add all remaining ingredients **(EXCEPT FOR CAULIRICE)** and

bring to a low boil. Cook for about 10-15 minutes or until it's hot all the way through.

OPTIONAL COOKING METHOD:

Slow cooker: Add all ingredients **(EXCEPT FOR CAULIRICE)** to slow cooker, and cook on low for 8 hours or high for 4 hours

Instant Pot: Add all ingredients **(EXCEPT FOR CAULIRICE)** to Instant Pot, and cook on manual time setting for 30 minutes.

CLUB SANDWICH

SERVES: 4

PER SERVING

CALORIES: 550

FAT: 28G

PROTEIN: 35G

CARBS: 5G

FIBER: 1G

Ingredients:

- 4 ea 90 second bread recipe OR 8 slices keto friendly bread

- Ham, deli meat

- Turkey, deli meat

- 8 slices bacon

- 4 slices Swiss cheese

- 4 slices cheddar cheese

- Lettuce, tomato, mayo, mustard

Directions:

1. Make each of the 90 second breads, slice in half to make a top and bottom portion of the bread for each sandwich and toast each one

2. Assemble sandwiches and enjoy

3. Easy peasy!

COBB SALAD

SERVES: 4

PER SERVING

CALORIES: 585

FAT: 52G

PROTEIN: 22G

CARBS: 14G

FIBER: 8G

Ingredients:

- 1 head Iceberg lettuce, chopped, washed & drained

- 10 slices bacon, cooked & chopped

- 2 chicken breasts, grilled & chopped (can use a rotisserie chicken)

- 4 boiled eggs

- 2 avocados, peeled & cubed

- 1 cup shredded cheese

- 2/3 cup cherry tomatoes

- 1 cucumber, peeled and chopped

- Ranch dressing (see Ranch Dressing recipe)

Directions:

1. Assemble salads in individual plates and distribute ingredients equally. Easy peasy!

CORN DOG BAKE

SERVES: 6

PER SERVING

CALORIES: 378

FAT: 36G

PROTEIN: 18G

CARBS: 6G

FIBER: 2.5G

Ingredients:

- 2 1/2 cups almond flour
- 1 1/2 cups shredded cheddar cheese
- 8 TBS butter, melted
- 2 1/2 tsp baking powder
- 1/2 tsp salt
- 2 TBS heavy whipping cream
- 4 TBS sweetener
- 6 eggs
- 4 TBS sour cream

- 1/4 cup jalapeños, drained
- 8 hot dogs, chopped
- Sugar free ketchup and mustard **FOR TOPPING**

Directions:

1. Preheat oven to 425°F

2. In a mixing bowl, combine all ingredients

3. Pour mixture into a greased 8 or 9 inch baking dish (or lined with parchment paper) and spread it out.

4. Bake for 18-22 minutes minutes, or until top is golden.

5. Remove from oven, allow to cook for a few minutes.

6. Cut into squares, and top with ketchup and mustard.

CORNBREAD MUFFINS

SERVES: 9 MUFFINS

PER SERVING

CALORIES: 154

FAT: 14G

PROTEIN: 6G

CARBS: 2G

FIBER: 1G

Ingredients:

- 1 1/4 cup almond flour
- 3/4 cup shredded cheddar cheese
- 4 TBS salted butter, melted
- 1 1/4 tsp baking powder
- 1/4 tsp salt
- 1 TBS heavy whipping cream
- 2 TBS sweetener
- 3 eggs
- 2 TBS sour cream

OPTIONAL MIX-IN

Diced jalapeños

Directions:

1. Preheat oven to 450°F

2. In a mixing bowl, combine all ingredients

3. In a muffin tin, add muffin liners and spray with nonstick spray.

4. Spoon batter into each one

5. Bake for 13-15 minutes

6. Best served warm and slathered with butter!

CREAMY ALFREDO

SERVES: 8

PER SERVING

CALORIES: 230

FAT: 23G

PROTEIN: 3G

CARBS: 2G

FIBER: 0G

Ingredients:

- 2 TBS butter

- 2 TBS minced garlic

- 2 TBS cream cheese

- 1 1/2 cups heavy whipping cream

- 1/2 cup Parmesan Cheese (I use kraft or great value brand in the jar)

- 1/2 tsp pepper

- 1/2 tsp parsley

- 2 packs Natural Heaven pasta, **_OR_** 2 packs Pasta Zero, **_OR_** 2 cups spaghetti squash

Directions:

1. In a saucepan, over low heat, add butter, garlic, cream cheese, heavy whipping cream, Parmesan cheese, pepper, and parsley.

2. Whisk to combine all ingredients, but DO NOT boil.

3. As soon as everything is melted and well combined, turn off heat and pour over pasta.

CREAMY BUFFALO SOUP

SERVES: 6

PER SERVING

CALORIES: 414

FAT: 30G

PROTEIN: 30G

CARBS: 7G

FIBER: 2G

Ingredients:

- 1 1/2 lbs chicken breast, cubed **OR** a rotisserie chicken
- 4 TBS avocado oil **OR** butter
- 1/4 tsp cajun seasoning
- 1 1/2 tsp parsley
- 1/2 tsp garlic powder
- 5 cups chicken broth or stock
- 1/2 cup celery, chopped
- 3 oz cream cheese, cubed
- 1 cup shredded cheddar cheese
- 1/2 cup half & half
- 1/4 cup Parmesan cheese
- 1/3 cup creamy buffalo ranch sauce (I like Moore's)
- Green onion, shopped for GARNISH

Directions:

1. In a pot, over medium heat, add oil, chicken breast, powdered seasonings and celery.
2. Cook until chicken is done and celery is tender.
3. Reduce heat and add all of the remaining ingredients
4. Simmer until cheese is melted, and it's heated throughout.

Optional cooking methods:

Slow cooker: Add all ingredients to slow cooker, and cook on low for 8 hours or high for 4 hours

Instant Pot: Add all ingredients to Instant Pot and set manual time for 30 minutes or set on "Soup" setting

EGG ROLL IN A BOW

SERVES: 4

PER SERVING

CALORIES: 202

FAT: 15G

PROTEIN: 27G

CARBS: 8G

FIBER: 3G

Ingredients:

- 1 pound ground pork
- 3 TBS avocado oil
- 1 (16 oz bag) coleslaw mix
- 1/2 cup onion, chopped
- 1 TBS sesame oil
- 2 tsp minced garlic
- 3 TBS soy sauce OR coconut aminos
- 1/2 tsp salt
- 1/2 tsp pepper
- 1/4 tsp onion powder

Directions:

1. In a skillet, heat oil and cook pork with chopped onion, salt, pepper, and onion powder.

2. Add coleslaw mix with remaining ingredients.

3. Cook and stir until tender.

4. Remove from heat, and serve.

FAJITA BOWL

SERVES: 4

PER SERVING

CALORIES: 862

FAT: 67G

PROTEIN: 19G

CARBS: 9G

FIBER: 2G

Ingredients:

- 1 1/2 pounds boneless skinless chicken thighs
- 3 TBS avocado oil
- 1 onion, sliced
- 1 bell pepper, sliced
- 1/2 tsp pepper
- 1/4 tsp salt
- 1 tsp chili powder
- 1 tsp cumin
- 1 tsp paprika
- Lettuce (your favorite kind, I use iceberg)
- 1/2 cup tomatoes, chopped
- 2 avocados, cubed
- 1 cup Cheese (your favorite blend)
- 1 cup Sour cream
- Sour Cream drizzle, optional (see Sour Cream Drizzle recipe)

Directions:

1. In a skillet, heat oil, add chicken, onions, peppers, and seasonings.

2. Cook thoroughly and remove from heat.

3. Divide lettuce, tomatoes, avocados, cheese and sour cream between 4 servings and top with chicken, onions and peppers.

4. Enjoy!

FAJITA CHICKEN CASSEROLE

SERVES: 4

PER SERVING

CALORIES: 211

FAT: 13G

PROTEIN: 21G

CARBS: 5.5G

FIBER: 2G

Ingredients:

- 4 chicken breasts, sliced into strips
- 1 green bell pepper, sliced
- 1 red bell pepper, sliced
- 1 onion, sliced
- 1 tsp cumin
- 1 TBS chili powder
- 1 tsp garlic powder
- 1 1/2 tsp paprika
- 1/2 tsp salt
- 1/4 tsp pepper
- 2 cups Mexican blend cheese, shredded

Garnish

Sour cream, avocado, olives, lettuce, tomato, guacamole

Directions:

1. Preheat oven to 400°F

2. In a 9x13 baking dish, place chicken breasts and coat with powdered seasonings.

3. Top with bell pepper, onion and shredded cheese.

4. Bake for 20-25 minutes.

FAUX REFRIED BEANS

SERVES: 4

PER SERVING

CALORIES: 101

FAT: 7G

PROTEIN: 5G

CARBS: 6G

FIBER: 2G

Ingredients:

- 1 Large eggplant
- 1 zucchini
- 3 strips bacon, cut up
- 1/2 cup onion, chopped
- 1 TBS chili powder
- 1 tsp paprika
- 1 tsp cumin
- 1/2 tsp salt
- 1/2 tsp pepper

- 4 TBS butter

Directions:

1. Peel the eggplant and zucchini and chop into cubes

2. In a skillet over medium heat, add butter, onions, bacon, eggplant, and zucchini

3. Add seasonings and cook down until it's all fork tender

4. Remove it all from the pan, put in a bowl or measuring cup and use a food processor, or immersion blender and blend it until it's smooth.

FRENCH DIP SANDWICH

SERVES: 4

PER SERVING

CALORIES: 327

FAT: 18G

PROTEIN: 27G

CARBS: 3G

FIBER: 0G

Ingredients:

"Bread" Chaffle ingredients

- 4 eggs

- 3/4 cup mozzarella cheese

- 1/4 cup cheddar cheese

- 1/2 tsp baking powder

- 1/4 tsp garlic powder

- 1/4 tsp onion powder

Fillings/Toppings

- 1 lb roast beef, shredded & heated

- 4 slices, mozzarella cheese

- 1/2 cup beef broth

- Optional condiments, mayo, Dijon mustard, grilled onions, grilled peppers

Directions:

1. Preheat waffle iron & oven at 350 degrees

2. In a mixing bowl, combine all of "Bread" ingredients and spoon into waffle iron. Mixture will make 8 pieces of "bread"

3. Fill each sandwich with meat and top with cheese.

4. Place on baking sheet and put in the oven for 3-5 minutes, or until cheese is melted.

5. Remove from oven and add toppings, i.e. mayo, mustard onions and peppers

6. Slice sandwiches and dip in warmed up beef broth.

GARLIC PORK CHOPS

SERVES: 4

PER SERVING

CALORIES: 575

FAT: 40G

PROTEIN: 44G

CARBS: 7G

FIBER: 1.5G

Ingredients:

Pork Chops:

- 4 pork chops, thick cut, bone-in (about 1/2" to 1" inch thick)
- 1/4 tsp salt
- 1/4 tsp pepper
- 1/4 tsp Cajun seasoning
- 1/2 tsp garlic powder
- 3 TBS butter

Sauce:

- 1 cup mushrooms, sliced
- 2 TBS minced garlic
- 1 tsp Italian seasoning
- 1 1/2 cups heavy whipping cream
- 1/2 cup chicken broth
- 1 TBS parsley
- Sprinkle of salt & pepper, to taste

Directions:

Pork Chops

1. Season both sides of pork chops with salt, pepper, Cajun seasoning, and garlic powder.

2. In a skillet, melt butter and add pork chops.

3. On a medium-high heat, sear both sides of chops for 3 minutes per side.

4. Remove from skillet, and reduce heat.

Sauce

1. In the same skillet, add mushrooms, and cook until they are tender.

2. Add all of the remaining "Sauce" ingredients and bring to a low simmer.

3. Place pork chops back into the pan with the sauce.

4. Enjoy!

GENERAL TSO'S CHICKEN

SERVES: 4

PER SERVING

CALORIES: 343

FAT: 38G

PROTEIN: 55G

CARBS: 7G

FIBER: 2G

Ingredients:

CHICKEN INGREDIENTS:

- 6-7 Boneless skinless chicken thighs
- 3/4 cup crushed pork rinds
- 1/3 cup Parmesan cheese
- 2 eggs
- 1/2 cup heavy whipping cream
- Oil for frying

SAUCE:

- 1 cup chicken broth
- 3 TBS rice vinegar
- 3 TBS soy sauce
- 2 TBS sugar free ketchup
- 3 TBS sweetener
- 1 1/2 tsp sesame oil
- 1 tsp coconut OR liquid aminos
- 1 tsp tomato paste
- 1 tsp red chili pepper flakes
- 1 tsp garlic powder
- 1 tsp minced garlic
- 1 tsp ginger paste
- Sprinkle of xanthan gum or guar gum (to thicken sauce up)
- Garnish with green onion & sesame seeds, optional

Directions:

1. Cut chicken into small pieces.

2. In a bowl, mix crushed pork rinds and Parmesan cheese.

3. In a separate bowl, whisk eggs and heavy whipping cream.

4. Add chicken pieces to this bowl.

5. Next, coat chicken in pork rind/Parmesan cheese mixture, and set aside.

6. In a pan, add oil and heat over medium high heat.

7. Fry chicken pieces and remove once they're cooked.

- **OR IF YOU DON'T WANT TO DEEP FRY THE PIECES, YOU CAN COOK THEM IN AN AIR FRYER.**

- **Place coated chicken pieces in air fryer on 375 for 15-18 minutes or until cooked.**

8. Place on a rack to drain off grease.

9. In a saucepan, over medium heat, add all "SAUCE" ingredients **(EXECPT for xanthan gum)** and bring to a low simmer.

10. Cook sauce for 5-7 minutes.

11. Remove from heat.

12. Add xanthan gum and whisk to thicken sauce.

13. Now that your chicken and sauce are cooked, coat chicken with sauce and serve.

GREEN CHILE CHICKEN ENCHILADAS

SERVES: 8

PER SERVING

CALORIES: 655

FAT: 35G

PROTEIN: 25G

CARBS: 9G

FIBER: 3G

Ingredients:

- 3 boneless, skinless chicken breasts (cooked & shredded), OR a rotisserie chicken
- 3/4 cup chicken broth
- 1/4 tsp onion powder
- 1/2 tsp chili powder
- 1/2 tsp paprika
- 1/2 tsp salt
- 1/2 tsp pepper
- 1 tsp cumin
- 1 (10 oz) can green chile enchilada sauce
- 1/2 cup heavy whipping cream
- 1 (12 oz) bag frozen riced cauliflower, steamed
- 1/3 cup sour cream
- 1 1/2 cups pepper jack cheese, shredded
- 1 cup cheddar cheese, shredded
- 1 cup Mexican Blend cheese, shredded FOR TOPPING
- 4 low carb tortillas

Directions:

1. Preheat oven to 350°F

2. In a small large bowl, mix all of the ingredients, **EXCEPT** for tortillas and Mexican blend cheese

3. In a 9x13 baking dish lay out 2 of the low carb tortillas

4. Add the chicken, cheese mixture on top

5. Top with the two remaining low carb tortillas, and the Mexican cheese blend

6. Bake for 20-22 minutes, or until cheese is melted & bubbly

OPTIONAL TOPPINGS:

Sour cream, lettuce, tomato, guacamole, tomatoes, jalapeños, cilantro

GRILLED AVOCADOS

SERVES: 4

PER SERVING

CALORIES: 201

FAT: 17G

PROTEIN: 2.4G

CARBS: 9G

FIBER: 6G

Ingredients:

Avocados

- 4 Avocados
- Pico de Gallo
- Chili lime seasoning, to taste
- Sour Cream drizzle
- Avocado oil, or olive oil

SOUR CREAM DRIZZLE:

- 1/4 cup sour cream
- 1/4 tsp chili powder
- 1 TBS water

Directions:

1. Preheat griddle.
2. Cut avocados in half, and remove seed.
3. Drizzle the inside of each avocado with oil and sprinkle with chili lime seasoning.
4. Place each one face down on the griddle.
5. Cook for about 3-4 minutes.
6. You just want them to have a nice sear/ grill mark on them.
7. Remove from heat.
8. Top each grilled avocado with Pico de gallo and sour cream drizzle

Sour Cream Drizzle

9. Put all of the 'SOUR CREAM DRIZZLE' ingredients in a ziploc bag.
10. Shake it all up to get in mixed well.
11. Cut off a tiny part of the edge (you're making a piping bag out of this)

HAM & CHEESE BAKE

SERVES: 4

PER SERVING

CALORIES: 535

FAT: 40G

PROTEIN: 29G

CARBS: 7G

FIBER: 2G

Ingredients:

- 2 lbs thick cut ham OR Ham Steak, cubed

- 1 (12 oz) bag frozen broccoli, steamed & drained

- 5 oz cream cheese, room temp & cubed

- 1/2 cup mayo

- 1 1/2 TBS Dijon mustard

- 1/2 TBS Worcestershire sauce

- 2 TBS sweetener

- 2 TBS heavy whipping cream

- 4 slices Swiss cheese, broken up into pieces

- 1/2 cup cheddar cheese, shredded, **FOR TOPPING**

Directions:

1. Preheat oven to 375°F

2. In a mixing bowl, combine cream cheese, mayo, and heavy whipping cream. It's easiest to do this if all ingredients are room temp.

3. Add all of the remaining ingredients and mix well.

4. Transfer mixture to 8 inch baking dish.

5. Top with cheddar cheese.

6. Bake for 20 minutes, or until cheese is melted and bubbly on top.

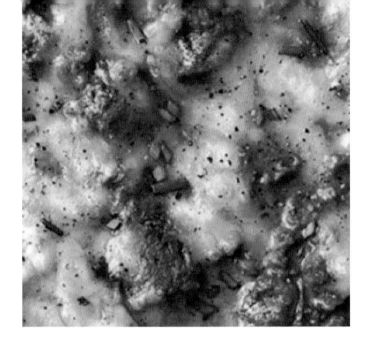

HAMBURGER ASSISTAN

SERVES: 6

PER SERVING

CALORIES: 388

FAT: 20G

PROTEIN: 40G

CARBS: 12G

FIBER: 4G

Ingredients:

- 1 lb ground beef
- 1/2 cup onions, chopped
- 1/2 tsp garlic powder
- 1 tsp salt
- 1/2 tsp pepper
- 1 tsp paprika
- 3 TBS tomato paste
- 1 tsp mustard

- 2 TBS parsley
- 1/3 cup heavy whipping cream
- 1/2 cup beef broth
- 1 tsp sweetener
- 1 1/2 cups shredded cheddar cheese
- 2 packs Pasta Zero **OR** Natural Heaven Pasta, OR Spaghetti squash **WHICHEVER ONE YOU USE,** cut them into 1 inch sections. This gives the meal a great texture!

Directions:

1. In a large skillet, cook beef and onions seasoned with garlic powder, salt, pepper, paprika, parsley, and sweetener.

2. When the meat is browned, reduce heat and add the remaining ingredients.

3. Stir well and let this simmer on low until the cheese is melted, and everything is heated throughout.

HAMBURGER STEAK

SERVES: 6

PER SERVING

CALORIES: 232

FAT: 20G

PROTEIN: 23G

CARBS: 2G

FIBER: 1G

Ingredients:

PATTIES INGREDIENTS

- 2 pounds ground beef
- 2 eggs
- 1/2 tsp salt
- 1/2 tsp pepper
- 1/2 tsp Cajun seasoning
- 1/2 tsp onion powder
- 1/2 tsp garlic powder

- 1/4 cup onion, chopped
- 1/4 cup bell pepper, chopped

GRAVY INGREDIENTS

- 1 1/2 cup beef broth
- 1/4-1 tsp guar gum or xanthan gum

Directions:

1. In a mixing bowl, combine all of the ingredients for the patties and combine well.

2. Form into 6 equal patties.

3. In a preheated skillet, cook patties until they are to your desired doneness.

4. Remove from pan and set aside.

5. Using the drippings that remain in the skillet, lower heat to a low setting.

6. Pour in beef broth and deglaze the drippings from the skillet bottom.

7. Sprinkle in thickener (guar gum or xanthan gum) and whisk until it's dissolved.

8. Add patties back into gravy.

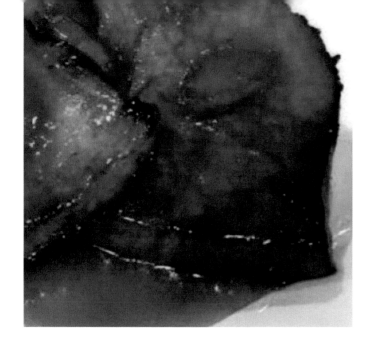

"HONEY" GLAZED HAM

SERVES: 4

PER SERVING

CALORIES: 342

FAT: 23G

PROTEIN: 29G

CARBS: 1G

FIBER: 0G

Ingredients:

- 2 lbs ham steak
- 5 TBS butter, room temp

Glaze Ingredients:

- 1/4 cup water
- 4 TBS sugar free syrup
- 4 TBS Dijon mustard
- 2 TBS sweetener
- 1/2 TBS apple cider vinegar
- 1 tsp pumpkin pie spice

Directions:

1. Preheat oven to 325°F
2. In a 9x13 baking pan, lay ham steaks and rub with butter
3. In a small dish, combine all "Glaze" Ingredients and mix until it's combined.
4. Pour the "Glaze" mixture over ham steaks
5. Bake in oven for 15-20 minutes.

ITALIAN DRESSING

SERVES: 1.5 CUPS

PER 2 TBS SERVING

CALORIES: 15

FAT: 1G

PROTEIN: 0G

CARBS: 0G

FIBER: 1G

Ingredients:

- 1 cup **EXTRA LIGHT TASTING** olive oil
- 1/2 cup white vinegar
- 1 tsp basil, dried
- 1/2 tsp oregano
- 1/4 tsp salt
- 1/4 tsp pepper
- 1 TBS minced garlic
- 1/4 tsp onion powder
- 1/2 tsp lemon juice
- 2 TBS Parmesan cheese

Directions:

1. In a blender, combine all ingredients, and blend on high until it's fully emulsified.

2. Let the dressing rest for a bit before using, but it's not a big deal if you use it immediately.

3. Store in the refrigerator for up to 2 weeks.

ITALIAN STYLE SALAD

SERVES: 4

PER SERVING

CALORIES: 30

FAT: 0G

PROTEIN: 2G

CARBS: 3G

FIBER: 1G

Ingredients:

- 1 (12 oz) bag iceberg garden salad

- 1/4 red onion, sliced thin

- 12 black olives, whole

- 6 pepperoncini peppers, mild

- 2 Roma tomatoes, sliced

- Parmesan cheese

- **_RECIPE FOR ITALIAN DRESSING_**

Directions:

1. Put all of the ingredients in a bowl and mix well to coat it all with the dressing

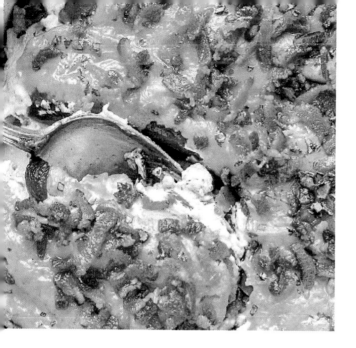

JALAPEÑO POPPER CASSEROLE

SERVES: 8

PER SERVING

CALORIES: 445

FAT: 32G

PROTEIN: 32G

CARBS: 3G

FIBER: .5G

Ingredients:

- 2 lbs chicken, cooked & shredded (can use white or dark meat)

  - **OR** you can use a rotisserie chicken, shredded

- 8 oz cream cheese, cubed, and softened

- 3/4 cup chicken broth

- 1/2 cup heavy whipping cream

- 1 cup sharp cheddar cheese, shredded

- 1/4-1/2 cup sliced jalapeños (I use the ones in the jar, drained)

- 1/2 tsp onion powder

- 1/2 tsp garlic powder

- 1/2 tsp paprika

- 1/2 tsp pepper

- 6 slices bacon, cooked & crumbled

- 1 cup Colby **OR** Monterey Jack cheese

Directions:

1. Preheat oven to 350 degrees

2. In a bowl combine chicken, cream cheese, broth, cream, cheddar cheese, jalapeños, garlic powder, onion powder, paprika, pepper, and bacon.

3. Transfer mixture to 9x13 baking dish and top with Colby **OR** Monterey Jack cheese.

4. Bake for 10-15 minutes, or until cheese is melted and bubbly.

JALAPEÑO POPPER CHICKEN

SERVES: 4

PER SERVING

CALORIES: 464

FAT: 29G

PROTEIN: 45G

CARBS: 3G

FIBER: 0G

Ingredients:

- 4 chicken breasts
- 1/4 tsp salt
- 1/4 tsp pepper
- 1/4 tsp Cajun seasoning
- 1/4 tsp garlic powder
- 1/4 tsp onion powder
- 6 oz cream cheese, room temp
- 1/2 cup cheddar cheese, shredded

- 1/2 cup mozzarella cheese, shredded
- 4 strips bacon, cooked & chopped
- 2 TBS jalapeño, chopped (I use the ones in the jar)
- 1/2 cup cheddar cheese, reserved for topping

Directions:

1. Preheat oven to 400°F
2. Slice each breast horizontally (butterfly cut) and season them with salt, pepper, onion powder, garlic powder, and Cajun seasoning.
3. Set aside.
4. In a bowl mix cream cheese, shredded cheeses, bacon and jalapeño pieces.
5. Stuff each breast with equal amounts of mixture and "close breasts and place in baking dish.
6. Sprinkle with remaining cheddar cheese.
7. Bake for approximately 25 minutes.

JAMBALAYA SOUP

SERVES: 12

PER SERVING

CALORIES: 480

FAT: 36G

PROTEIN: 33G

CARBS: 13G

FIBER: 4G

Ingredients:

- 5 TBS avocado oil or butter
- 2 1/2 lbs boneless skinless chicken thighs
- 1 lb smoked sausage, sliced
- 2 lbs shrimp, cleaned and deveined
- 1 bunch green onion, sliced

- 2 TBS minced garlic
- 1/2 cup onion, chopped
- 1/2 cup bell pepper, chopped
- 1/2 cup celery, chopped
- 1 cup cut okra, (I prefer frozen)
- 1 tsp salt
- 1 tsp pepper

- 2 tsps cajun seasoning
- 1 TBS parsley
- 2 tsp crab boil
- 1 (14.5) can crushed or diced tomatoes
- 4 cups chicken broth
- 1 (10 oz) bag riced cauliflower, steamed and drained

Directions:

1. In a large pot, over medium heat, add oil, chicken, sausage, shrimp green onion, garlic, onion, bell pepper, celery, and okra.

2. Cook until chopped seasonings are tender and shrimp are cooked.

3. Add all of the remaining ingredients **EXCEPT FOR CAULIFLOWER**.

4. Bring to a **low** boil, and cook for about 15 minutes or until everything is heated through.

5. Remove from heat and serve over steamed cauliflower rice.

JAPANESE HIBACHI SOUP

SERVES: 6

PER SERVING

CALORIES: 150

FAT: 4G

PROTEIN: 2G

CARBS: 1G

FIBER: 0G

Ingredients:

- 8 cups beef broth or stock
- 4 TBS butter
- 1/2 tsp salt
- 1/2 tsp pepper
- 1/2 cup onion, chopped
- 2 stalks celery, finely diced
- 2 TBS minced garlic
- 1 (8 oz) container fresh mushrooms

- 2 stalks green onion, chopped

Directions:

1. In a large pot, cook butter, onions, and celery. Cook until they are tender.

2. Add beef stock, garlic, salt, pepper and mushrooms.

3. Bring to a low simmer and cook for 10 minutes.

4. Remove from heat, garnish with green onions and serve.

LASAGNA

SERVES: 6

PER SERVING

CALORIES: 514

FAT: 28G

PROTEIN: 21G

CARBS: 8G

FIBER: 3G

Ingredients:

- 2 pounds ground beef
- 1 1/2 jars marinara/spaghetti sauce (no sugar added)
- 1/2 tsp salt
- 1/2 tsp pepper
- 1/2 tsp garlic powder
- 1/2 tsp onion powder
- 2 tsp Italian seasoning

- 1 cup ricotta cheese
- 2 cups mozzarella cheese
- 1 cup cheddar cheese
- Parmesan cheese, garnish
- OPTIONAL pasta substitute Natural Heaven, OR spaghetti squash

Directions:

1. Preheat oven to 350°F
2. Pasta substitute, optional, I love Natural Heaven lasagna noodles, or you could use thinly sliced eggplant.
3. This dish can be prepared WITHOUT a pasta substitute and still be just as delicious!
4. In a large pot, cook ground meat with seasonings.
5. Add sauce.
6. Simmer for a few minutes and remove from heat.
7. In a 9x13 baking pan layer all ingredients until the last layer on top is cheese.
8. Bake until the cheese on top is bubbly and melted well.

LASAGNA PEPPERS

SERVES: 8

PER SERVING

CALORIES: 207

FAT: 13G

PROTEIN: 19G

CARBS: 10G

FIBER: 3G

Ingredients:

- 4 bell peppers, stems & seeds removed, and sliced in half, lengthwise
- 2 lb ground beef
- 1/2 tsp salt
- 1/2 tsp pepper
- 1/2 tsp cajun seasoning
- 1/2 tsp onion powder
- 1/2 tsp garlic powder

- 1 TBS Italian seasoning
- 1 tsp parsley
- 1/2 cup Parmesan cheese
- 2 TBS sweetener
- 2 1/2 cup pasta/marinara sauce
- 1 cup ricotta cheese
- 1 cup mozzarella cheese, shredded

Directions:

1. Preheat oven to 400°F

2. In a skillet, over medium heat, cook beef seasoned with salt, pepper, cajun seasoning, onion powder, garlic powder, Italian seasoning, and parsley.

3. When the seasoned meat is cooked, add sauce, Parmesan cheese, and sweetener.

4. Lay out peppers in 9x13 baking dish

5. Spoon equal amounts of the meat sauce into each half pepper (approx 1/4 cup)

6. Add a layer of ricotta cheese to each pepper (approx 2 TBS)

7. Top with mozzarella cheese

8. Bake for 12-15 minutes, or until cheese is melted and bubbly

LOADED BROCCOLI

SERVES: 4

PER SERVING

CALORIES: 220

FAT: 19G

PROTEIN: 9G

CARBS: 5G

FIBER: 3G

Ingredients:

- 1 (12 oz) Broccoli florets, frozen

- 1 cup shredded cheddar cheese, shredded

- 1/3 cup sour cream

- 1/2 cup bacon, cooked and crumbled

- Green onion, garnish

- Salt & pepper, to taste

Directions:

1. Steam broccoli according to directions on bag.

2. Drain liquid.

3. Divide broccoli between four servings/ plates and top with cheese, sour cream, bacon, salt, pepper and green onion.

LOADED PIZZA BAKE

SERVES: 8

PER SERVING

CALORIES: 475

FAT: 35G

PROTEIN: 28G

CARBS: 9G

FIBER: 2G

Ingredients:

- 1 lb Italian sausage, cooked and broken up
- 6 slices smoked ham/deli style, chopped
- 1/2 cup red onion, chopped
- 1 (8 oz) mushrooms, sliced
- 1/2 cup bell pepper, diced
- 1 (21 oz) pkg pepperoni slices
- 1/2 cup black olives, sliced & drained
- 2 cups mozzarella cheese, shredded
- 1 jar (no sugar in ingredients list) marinara sauce (24 oz)
- Parmesan cheese, grated, for topping as garnish

Directions:

1. Preheat oven to 450°F

2. In a 9x13 baking dish, spread a thin layer of marinara sauce on the bottom.

3. Make several thin layers of each meat, vegetable, and sauce.

4. Top with mozzarella cheese.

5. Bake for 15-18 minutes, or until cheese is melted and bubbly.

MAC & CHEESE

SERVES: 6

PER SERVING

CALORIES: 330

FAT: 13G

PROTEIN: 15G

CARBS: 5G

FIBER: 2.1G

Ingredients:

- 2 packs Natural Heaven angel hair pasta OR 2 cups spaghetti squash OR Pasta Zero

- 1/4 cup butter, salted MELTED

- 4 TBS cream cheese ROOM TEMP

- 2 cups cheddar cheese, shredded

- 1/4-1/2 tsp salt

- 1/4-1/2 tsp pepper

- 1 tsp parsley

- 1/2 cup cheddar cheese, shredded (for topping)

Directions:

1. Preheat oven to 350°F

2. In a baking dish 9x13, or similar size, combine all ingredients EXCEPT for cheese topping.

3. Mix well and top with the shredded cheese that is designated for the topping.

4. Bake for 15 minutes, or until cheese is bubbly on top.

MAC DADDY CASSEROL

SERVES: 6

PER SERVING

CALORIES: 656

FAT: 51G

PROTEIN: 44G

CARBS: 6G

FIBER: 2G

Ingredients:

- 1 1/2 lbs ground beef
- 4 TBS cream cheese, room temp
- 3 TBS sugar free ketchup
- 1 TBS mustard
- 1 TBS Worcestershire sauce
- 2 TBS minced garlic
- 1 tsp salt
- 1 tsp pepper

- 1/2 tsp cajun seasoning
- 4 eggs, lightly beaten
- 1/4 cup heavy whipping cream
- 1/2 cup shredded cheddar cheese PLUS 1 cup additional for topping

Sauce:

- 1/2 cup mayo
- 2 TBS dill relish

- 2 tsp mustard
- 2 tsp vinegar (any variation works)
- 1/4 tsp onion powder
- 1/2 tsp paprika
- 1/2 tsp sweetener

Toppings:

Lettuce, pickles, onions, tomato

Directions:

1. Preheat Oven to 350°F

2. In a skillet, cook beef with salt, pepper, and cajun seasoning. Remove from heat

3. In a mixing bowl, add meat. Whisk in egg and heavy whipping cream, then add cream cheese, ketchup, mustard, Worcestershire sauce, garlic, cream and cheese until fully combined.

4. Pour mixture into 9 inch baking dish (I like to line mine with parchment paper)

5. Top with remaining shredded cheese

6. Bake in oven for 25-30 minutes, or until cheese is bubbly and golden.

7. While the casserole is baking, make the sauce.

8. In a small bowl, combine all **"Sauce"** ingredients and stir it up. Put it in the fridge until the casserole is finished.

9. Top each serving of the casserole with Sauce and Toppings. Enjoy!

MEAT LOVERS PIZZA

SERVES: 2

PER SERVING

CALORIES: 752

FAT: 56G

PROTEIN: 49G

CARBS: 9G

FIBER: 3G

Ingredients:

CRUST:

- 1 3/4 cup mozzarella cheese, shredded
- 3/4 cup almond flour
- 2 TBS cream cheese, room temp
- 1 egg
- Salt, to taste
- Garlic powder, to taste

TOPPINGS:

- 12 slices pepperoni
- 4 oz cooked breakfast sausage
- 2 oz ham
- 2 pieces bacon, crumbled
- 1/2 cup no sugar added marinara sauce
- 1/2 cup mozzarella cheese, shredded

YOU WILL NEED TO MAKE 2 OF THIS RECIPE TO EQUAL ENOUGH FOR 4 SERVINGS (3 SLICES PER SERVING) THIS RECIPE WILL MAKE 6 SLICES

Directions:

1. Preheat oven to 425°F

2. Mix the mozzarella and cream cheeses together in a microwave safe bowl.

3. Microwave for 1 minute, then stir.

4. When the cheeses are melted, add remaining "CRUST" ingredients.

5. Place dough between two sheets of parchment paper and roll out into a circular pizza shape.

6. Make fork holes all over the dough.

7. Slide the dough onto a baking pan

8. Bake for 10-12 minutes.

9. If you want it crispy on both sides, you can flip it over and use the underside to put the topping on.

10. Add sauce, toppings and cheese.

11. Put back in the oven for approximately 5 minutes to crisp it up and melt cheese.

12. Cut into 6 slices.

MEXICAN CORNBREAD

SERVES: 6

PER SERVING

CALORIES: 160

FAT: 15G

PROTEIN: 5G

CARBS: 2G

FIBER: 1G

Ingredients:

- 1 1/4 cup almond flour
- 3/4 cup shredded cheddar cheese
- 4 TBS butter, melted
- 1 1/4 tsp baking powder
- 1/4 tsp salt
- 1 TBS heavy whipping cream
- 2 TBS sweetener

- 3 eggs
- 2 TBS sour cream
- 1/4 cup jalapeños, drained (I use the ones in the jar)
- 2 stalks green onion, finely chopped
- 1/4 cup red bell pepper, finely diced

Directions:

1. Preheat oven 350°F
2. Grease or line 8 inch baking dish.
3. In a mixing bowl, combine all ingredients well.
4. Pour mixture into baking dish.
5. Bake for 20-25 minutes, or until top is golden.

MEXICAN PIZZA

SERVES: 4

PER SERVING

CALORIES: 255

FAT: 19G

PROTEIN: 20G

CARBS: 13G

FIBER: 7G

Ingredients:

- 4 low carb tortillas
- 1/4 cup oil
- 1 lb ground beef
- 1/2 tsp salt
- 1/2 tsp pepper
- 1 TBS chili powder
- 1/4 tsp onion powder

- 1 tsp cumin
- 1 tsp paprika
- 1 cup Mexican blend cheese
- SEE RECIPE FOR FAUX REFRIED BEANS

Toppings:

Lettuce, tomato, sour cream drizzle, guacamole, olives, jalapeños

Directions:

1. Preheat oven to 350°F

2. Prepare the "Faux Beans" recipe and set aside.

3. In a skillet, over medium heat, add oil and fry tortillas to make them crunchy. When they are slightly golden, remove from oil and set them on a paper towel to drain off the excess grease.

4. Cook ground beef with salt, pepper, chili powder, onion powder, cumin and paprika.

5. On each tortilla, layer beans, beef and cheese.

6. Bake in the oven for 3-5 minutes, or until cheese is melted. Remove from oven.

7. Add toppings and serve.

MUFFULETTA

SERVES: 4

PER SERVING

CALORIES: 659

FAT: 37G

PROTEIN: 31G

CARBS: 6G

FIBER: 1G

Ingredients:

BREAD INGREDIENTS

- 1 cup almond flour

- 2 tsp baking powder

- 2 tsp active yeast

- 1/2 stick salted butter, melted

- 2 eggs, beaten

- 1 TBS sweetener

- 1/8 cup coconut flour

- Sesame seeds (garnish on top of bread)

MEATS & CHEESE/FILLING

- 8 slices mozzarella cheese

- 7 oz salami

- 6 oz pepperoni slices

- 9 oz sliced ham

- 1/4 - 1/2 cup olive salad, drained

Directions:

1. Preheat oven to 350°F

2. In a mixing bowl, combine all "**BREAD INGREDIENTS**".

3. Pour into 8" or 9" round baking pan that's lined with parchment paper (the size of the pan is up to you, as far as how thick or thin you want each layer of bread.)

4. Sprinkle sesame seeds on top of the bread batter.

5. Bake for 15-20 minutes.

6. Remove from oven and take out of pan.

7. Slice in half so you now have a top and bottom bun.

8. Layer all of the **MEATS & CHEESE/FILLING** on bottom bun.

9. Put top bun on and put completed muffuletta in the oven to melt the cheese and warm up the meat.

10. This will take about 5-8 minutes.

11. Remove, cut into quarter sections and enjoy!

NACHOS SUPREME BAKE

SERVES: 4

PER SERVING

CALORIES: 984

FAT: 65G

PROTEIN: 49G

CARBS: 13G

FIBER: 3G

Ingredients:

- 1 pound ground beef
- 1 1/2 tsp chili powder
- 1 tsp cumin
- 1/2 tsp salt
- 1/2 tsp pepper
- 1/2 tsp paprika
- 1/8 tsp onion powder
- 1 1/2 cup cheddar cheese, shredded

- 1/4 cup enchilada sauce
- 1 bag pork rinds
- Optional toppings: Sour cream, avocado, olives, salsa, green onion, lettuce, tomatoes
- SEE FAUX BEAN RECIPE

Directions:

1. Preheat oven to 350°F

2. In a skillet, cook ground beef with seasonings.

3. Remove from heat and add enchilada sauce, mix well.

4. Transfer to 9" baking dish.

5. Top with "Faux Refried Beans" and cheese.

6. Bake in oven for 12-15 minutes.

7. Serve with optional toppings and pork rinds.

ORANGE CHICKEN

SERVES: 6

PER SERVING

CALORIES: 450

FAT: 22G

PROTEIN: 33G

CARBS: 8G

FIBER: 0G

Ingredients:

- 2 lbs boneless skinless chicken thighs, cubed

- 1 tsp salt

- 3 TBS coconut oil

SAUCE INGREDIENTS:

- 2 cups chicken broth

- 3 TBS sweetener

- 2 TBS Orange Blast or orange flavored liquid drink enhancer mix in

(Great Value or Crystal Light brand works) OR 1/4 cup no sugar added orange juice

- 1/2 tsp ginger paste

- 1/4 tsp red pepper flakes

- 1/4 tsp pepper

- 2 TBS minced garlic

- 3 TBS coconut aminos OR soy sauce

- 1/4 tsp toasted sesame oil

- 1 TBS sugar free ketchup

- Pinch of xanthan gum

- Sesame seeds, for **_topping_**

Directions:

1. In a skillet, over high heat add oil, chicken and salt.

2. Cook until chicken is done, then remove the pieces of chicken.

3. In the skillet, now add all of the "Sauce Ingredients"

4. Cook on medium-high heat, bringing it to a light boil.

5. Cook this down until it becomes a thicker consistency, like a glaze.

6. Reduce heat, add chicken back to the skillet and coat it in the sauce.

7. Turn off heat and serve.

PASTALAYA

SERVES: 6

PER SERVING

CALORIES: 520

FAT: 39G

PROTEIN: 41G

CARBS: 5G

FIBER: 1G

Ingredients:

- 2 lbs boneless skinless chicken thighs, cubed
- 1 (14 0z) pack smoked sausage, diced
- 1 can (14.5 oz) diced tomatoes, drained
- 1 bunch (5.5 oz) green onions, chopped
- 1/4 cup oil, or butter
- 1 tsp salt
- 2 tsp pepper
- 1 tsp cajun seasoning
- 1/2 tsp onion powder
- 2 tsp parsley
- 1/2 tsp garlic powder
- 1/4 cup parmesan cheese
- 1 cup heavy whipping cream
- 2 pks Pasta Zero OR Natural Heaven OR spaghetti squash

Directions:

1. In a skillet, over medium heat, add oil, chicken, sausage, tomatoes, and green onion.

2. Season with salt, pepper, cajun seasoning, onion powder, and garlic powder. Cook until chicken is done.

3. Lower heat and add parmesan cheese, heavy whipping cream and pasta "replacement"

4. Mix well to coat the pasta and simmer until it is warmed through. Remove from heat.

PEPPERONI PIZZA

SERVES: 4

PER SERVING

CALORIES: 251

FAT: 20G

PROTEIN: 17G

CARBS: 5G

FIBER: 2G

Ingredients:

CRUST INGREDIENTS:

- 1 large egg
- 2 cups mozzarella cheese
- 3/4 c. almond flour
- 3 TBS cream cheese, room temp
- 1/4 tsp salt
- 1/2 tsp garlic powder
- 1 tsp Italian seasoning

TOPPINGS:

- 3/4 c. low-carb sugar-free tomato sauce
- 1/2 c. thinly sliced pepperoni

Directions:

1. Preheat oven to 425°F.

2. Line a baking pan with parchment paper.

3. In a microwave safe bowl, 2 cups mozzarella and cream cheese.

4. Once melted, add almond flour, eggs, and seasonings.

5. Mix until well combined.

6. Spread mixture evenly in a circle (10-12 inches) on prepared sheet tray.

7. Bake until lightly golden, about 10 minutes.

8. Turn crust upside down

9. Spread pizza sauce on top of baked crust.

10. Top with mozzarella, and pepperoni.

11. Bake until cheese is melty and crust is crisp, approximately 15 minutes

PHILLY CHEESESTEAK CASSEROLE

SERVES: 6

PER SERVING

CALORIES: 355

FAT: 22G

PROTEIN: 34G

CARBS: 6G

Ingredients:

- 2 pounds ground beef

- 1 1/2 cups bell pepper, chopped (I like to use red & green peppers)

- 1 cup onion, chopped

- 2 TBS oil (avocado or olive oil)

- 1 tsp salt

- 1 tsp pepper

- 1/2 tsp Cajun seasoning

- 1/2 tsp garlic powder

- 1 1/2 tsp Worcestershire sauce

- 1/4 cup heavy cream

- 3 eggs

- 2 cups shredded mozzarella, Swiss, or provolone cheese (Topping)

Directions:

1. Preheat oven to 350°F

2. In a skillet with oil, add beef, onions, peppers, salt, pepper, Cajun seasoning, garlic powder, and Worcestershire sauce.

3. When meat is finished cooking remove from heat and transfer to baking dish (9x13 or similar size)

4. In a measuring cup whisk eggs and heavy cream.

5. Pour mixture into baking dish and mix well.

6. Top with cheese and bake for 15 minutes, or until cheese is bubbly on top.

7. Enjoy!

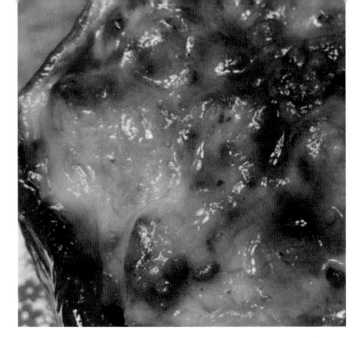

PHILLY CHEESESTEAK PEPPERS

SERVES: 4

PER SERVING

CALORIES: 395

FAT: 30G

PROTEIN: 24G

CARBS: 6G

FIBER: 1G

Ingredients:

- 2 TBS avocado oil or Butter

- 16 oz shredded roast beef, sliced

- 3 bell peppers, 2 halved and seeded, one seeded and sliced into strips

- 1/2 yellow onion, sliced thin

- 1/4 tsp salt

- 1/4 tsp pepper

- 1/4 tsp cajun seasoning

- 1/4 tsp garlic powder

- 1/2 cup mozzarella cheese, shredded

- 4 sliced Swiss cheese

Directions:

If you use a cast iron skillet, this is a one pot meal

1. Preheat oven to 400°F

2. In a skillet, add oil, roast beef, onion, bell pepper strips, salt, pepper, cajun seasoning, and garlic powder.

3. Cook until the onions and peppers are just getting tender and add shredded mozzarella. Stir and remove from heat.

4. If you didn't use a cast iron skillet, you'll need a baking dish. Either way, you'll need to take this mixture and stuff it in the peppers that you halved earlier.

5. Top each pepper with a slice of Swiss cheese

6. Bake for 15 minutes.

PORK LOIN

SERVES: 6

PER SERVING

CALORIES: 264

FAT: 15G

PROTEIN: 23G

CARBS: 1G

FIBER: 1G

Ingredients:

- 1 1/2-2 pound pork loin
- 1 tsp salt
- 1 tsp pepper
- 1/2 tsp Cajun seasoning
- 1/4 cup onions, chopped
- 1/4 tsp garlic powder
- 8 TBS butter, cubed

- **OPTIONAL**: If you want a creamy gravy, you can add a splash of heavy whipping cream to the gravy and a a sprinkle of guar or xanthan gum.

Directions:

Oven method:

1. Preheat oven to 400°F

2. Place pork in a baking pan, and sprinkle with seasonings and butter.

3. Cover with foil and bake for 45 minutes to an hour,

4. depending on your oven.

Crockpot method:

1. Add all ingredients to crockpot

2. Cook on low for 8 hours, or on high for 4 hours

Instant Pot method:

1. Add all ingredients to InstantPot

2. Set the manual time to 30 minutes.

PORK MEDALLIONS

SERVES: 4

PER SERVING

CALORIES: 387

FAT: 27G

PROTEIN: 35G

CARBS: 7G

FIBER: 2G

Ingredients:

- 1 ½ pound pork loin, cubed (½" pieces)
- 4 TBS avocado oil
- 1 medium onion, chopped
- ½ tsp. salt
- ½ tsp. pepper
- ½ tsp. cajun seasoning
- ½ tsp. Onion powder
- 1 tbs. minced garlic

CREAM SAUCE:

- 8 TBS butter
- 1 cup chicken broth
- 1/2 cup heavy whipping cream
- 1/2 tsp pepper
- 1 tsp parsley
- 1 TBS minced garlic
- Pinch of xanthan or guar gum, optional (thickening agent)

Directions:

1. In a large pot or skillet, on medium high heat, add oil and pork with powdered seasonings, and onion.

2. Seer pork pieces on all sides.

3. Reduce heat to low.

4. Add butter, broth, whipping cream, pepper, parsley and thickener.

5. Cover with lid and simmer on low for 30 minutes.

PORK RIND NACHOS

SERVES: 4

PER SERVING

CALORIES: 750

FAT: 55G

PROTEIN: 48G

CARBS: 10G

FIBER: 3G

Ingredients:

- 1 lb ground beef
- 1 1/2 tsp chili powder
- 1 tsp cumin
- 1/2 tsp salt
- 1/2 tsp pepper
- 1/2 tsp paprika
- 1/4 tsp onion powder
- 1 1/2 cup cheddar cheese, shredded

- 1 bag pork rinds
- Faux Refried Beans Recipe
- Sour Cream Drizzle Recipe
- Toppings: guacamole, salsa, olives, green onion, lettuce, tomatoes

Directions:

1. In a skillet, cook ground beef with powdered seasonings.

2. Make "Refried beans"

3. Start assembling nachos by making a bed of pork rinds, add "beans", meat, and toppings

RANCH BROCCOLI

SERVES: 4

PER SERVING

CALORIES: 146

FAT: 11G

PROTEIN: 4G

CARBS: 3G

FIBER: 3G

Ingredients:

- 2 1/2 cups broccoli florets (fresh)
- 1/4 cup ranch dressing
- 1/2 cup cheddar cheese
- 1/4 cup half & half
- 1/4 cup Parmesan cheese
- 1/4 tsp salt

Directions:

1. Preheat oven to 375°F
2. In a bowl, combine all ingredients to coat them well.
3. Transfer to an 8" baking pan, lined with parchment paper (easy clean up).
4. And bake for 30 minutes.

RANCH DRESSING

SERVES: 20

PER SERVING

CALORIES: 170

FAT: 14G

PROTEIN: 0G

CARBS: .5G

FIBER: 0G

Ingredients:

- 1 Egg
- 1 cup "light" olive oil
- 1 tablespoon lemon juice
- 2 tablespoons red wine vinegar
- 1/2 teaspoon salt
- 3/4 teaspoon pepper
- 1/2 teaspoon onion powder
- 1/2 teaspoon garlic powder

- 1/2 cup full fat canned unsweetened coconut milk
- 2 tsp parsley flakes

Directions:

1. Pour all ingredients into blender and pulse until well combined OR you can use an immersion blender.

2. Store in airtight container in refrigerator for up to a week.

ROASTED ASPARAGUS

SERVES: 4

PER SERVING

CALORIES: 123

FAT: 10.3G

PROTEIN: 3G

CARBS: 5.2G

FIBER: 2.4G

Ingredients:

- 1 bunch asparagus spears, trim bottoms
- 3 TBS avocado oil
- 2 TBS grated parmesan cheese
- 1/2 tsp salt
- 1/2 tsp pepper

Directions:

1. Preheat oven to 425°F
2. Line baking pan with parchment paper.
3. Lay asparagus out on the pan.
4. Drizzle with oil and sprinkle salt, pepper, and cheese evenly.
5. I use my hands at this point to roll them around so they're coated evenly.
6. Bake in oven for 12-15 minutes.

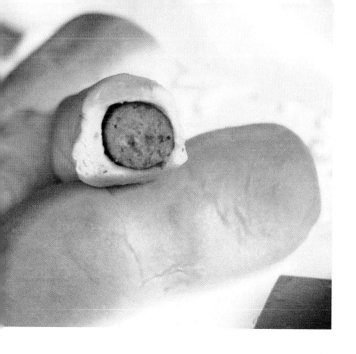

SAUSAGE & CHEESE KOLACHES

SERVES: 6

PER SERVING

CALORIES: 443

FAT: 28G

PROTEIN: 26G

CARBS: 10G

FIBER: 2G

Ingredients:

- 1 1/2 cup mozzarella cheese
- 3/4 cup almond flour
- 2 oz cream cheese
- 1 egg
- 1/2 TBS active dry yeast
- 1/2 TBS baking powder
- 1/2 TBS sweetener

- 6 Johnsonville Better with Cheddar Sausages

Directions:

1. Preheat oven to 400°F

2. In a microwave safe bowl, add mozzarella cheese and cream cheese.

3. Heat them up in 30 second increments, stirring in between.

4. When it's melted, add almond flour, yeast, baking powder, sweetener, and egg.

5. Mix to combine well.

6. Divide dough into 6 equal balls.

7. Wrap each dough ball around each sausage link and place on baking sheet.

8. Bake for 15-20 minutes, or until it's slightly golden on top.

SHRIMP SCAMPI

SERVES: 4

PER SERVING

CALORIES: 316

FAT: 17G

PROTEIN: 33G

CARBS: 4G

FIBER: 1G

Ingredients:

- 1 1/4 pounds shrimp, peeled & deveined
- 5 TBS butter
- 2 TBS minced garlic
- 1/2 cup seafood stock
- 2 TBS lemon juice
- 1/2 cup Parmesan cheese
- 1/2 tsp onion powder
- 1/2 tsp garlic powder
- 1/2 tsp parsley

- 1/2 tsp salt
- 1/2 tsp pepper
- 1/2 tsp Cajun seasoning
- 1 can (13.75 oz) artichoke hearts, drained
- 1/4 cup cherry tomatoes, sliced half
- 2 packs pasta substitute (I love Natural Heaven, but you can use Pasta Zero, or spaghetti squash)
- OPTIONAL: Sausage

Directions:

1. In a skillet over medium heat, add butter, shrimp, garlic, onion powder, garlic powder, parsley, salt, pepper, Cajun seasoning, artichoke hearts, and tomatoes.

2. Cook until shrimp are just turning pink.

3. Reduce heat and add seafood stock, Parmesan cheese, and lemon juice.

4. Add pasta substitute to skillet, and heat through.

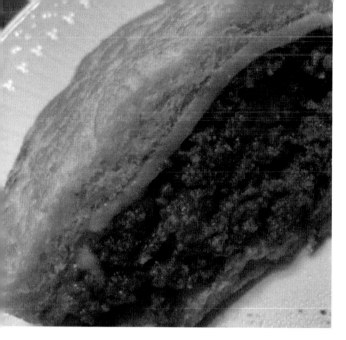

SLOPPY JOES

SERVES: 4

PER SERVING

CALORIES: 370

FAT: 28G

PROTEIN: 19G

CARBS: 8G

FIBER: 3G

Ingredients:

- 1 lb ground beef
- 1/2 cup bell pepper, chopped
- 1/4 cup onion, chopped
- 1/4 cup tomato paste
- 1 TBS sweetener
- 1 TBS sugar free maple or pancake syrup
- 1 TBS Dijon mustard
- 2 tsp apple cider vinegar
- 2 tsp Worcestershire sauce
- 1/2 cup beef broth

- 1/4 tsp salt
- 1/2 tsp pepper
- 1/4 tsp cajun seasoning
- 1/4 tsp garlic powder
- 1 TBS parsley
- 1/2 tsp Italian seasoning
- 4 slices cheddar cheese
- ***90 SECOND BREAD RECIPE (MAKE THIS 4 TIMES SO YOU HAVE ENOUGH FOR 4 SANDWICHES). OR YOU CAN USE SOLA BUNS***

Directions:

1. In a skillet, over medium heat, cook all ingredients until meat is cooked thoroughly and onions and peppers are tender.

2. Make 4 servings of the 90 second bread.

3. Assemble each sandwich with equal amounts of meat mixture and a slice of cheese each.

SMOTHERED BURRITOS

SERVES: 6

PER SERVING

CALORIES: 390

FAT: 20G

PROTEIN: 40G

CARBS: 11G

FIBER: 5G

Ingredients:

Burritos:

- 2 pounds ground beef
- 1 1/2 tsp salt
- 1 tsp pepper
- 2 TBS chili powder
- 1 1/2 tsp cumin
- 1 1/2 tsp paprika
- 1 cup shredded cheese, Fiesta blend (plus a little extra for topping)

- 6 low carb tortillas (I like Mission or Great Value brand)
- Optional garnishes, lettuce, tomato, black olives, sour cream, guacamole

Sauce:

- 3/4 cup heavy whipping cream

- 4 oz cream cheese, room temp
- 2 cups pepper jack cheese, shredded
- 1 cup Fiesta Blend cheese, shredded
- 4 TBS diced tomatoes
- Chili powder, to taste (approx 1/4-1/2 tsp)

Directions:

1. Preheat oven to 350 degrees

2. Make the "SAUCE" first.

3. In a microwave safe container (I like to use my Pyrex measuring cup) add all of the sauce ingredients.

4. In 30-60 second increments, heat it up until it's all melted.

5. Set aside.

6. In a skillet, brown ground beef with salt, pepper, chili powder, cumin & paprika.

7. Do NOT drain fat!

8. Now let's assemble the burritos!

9. Lay each tortilla out and fill with equal amounts of the meat mixture and shredded cheese.

10. Place them in a 9x13 baking dish.

11. Pour "SAUCE" on top and a little extra shredded cheese.

12. Bake for 10 minutes, or until cheese is melted and bubbly.

SMOTHERED CABBAGE

SERVES: 6

PER SERVING

CALORIES: 155

FAT: 11G

PROTEIN: 7.5G

CARBS: 5G

FIBER: 2.5G

Ingredients:

- 1 head cabbage, chopped and rinsed
- 1 lb smoked sausage, sliced
- 1/2 cup onion, chopped
- 5 TBS butter
- 1/2 tsp salt
- 1/2 tsp pepper
- 1/2 tsp Cajun seasoning
- 1/2 cup water

Directions:

1. In a large pot over medium heat, add onion, butter and sausage.

2. Cook this until onions are tender.

3. Add cabbage, salt, pepper, Cajun seasoning, and water and cover with lid.

4. Cook for 20 minutes and stir.

5. Turn heat up to medium high and put lid back on.

6. Cook for another 10 minutes, or until cabbage is tender.

SOUR CREAM CHICKE

SERVES: 4

PER SERVING

CALORIES: 269

FAT: 12G

PROTEIN: 40G

CARBS: 4G

FIBER: 0G

Ingredients:

- 4 chicken breasts
- 1/2 cup sour cream
- 4 TBS cream cheese
- 2 TBS heavy whipping cream
- 4 TBS butter, cubed
- 1 cup mozzarella cheese

- 1/2 cup cheddar cheese
- 1/4 cup Parmesan cheese
- 1/2 tsp salt
- 1/2 tsp pepper
- 1 tsp Italian seasoning
- Parsley, garnish

Directions:

1. Preheat oven to 350°F
2. If your chicken breasts are thick, butterfly cut (or slice in half) to thin them out
3. Lay chicken in baking dish.
4. In a measuring cup, combine cream cheese, heavy whipping cream, butter, parmesan cheese, and seasonings.
5. Melt this in the microwave and pour over chicken breasts in pan.
6. Top with mozzarella & cheddar cheese and bake for 35-45 minutes.

OPTIONAL COOKING METHODS:

InstantPot:

1. Add all ingredients to InstantPot.
2. Set manual time to 12 minutes
3. Do quick pressure release.

Crockpot:

1. Add all ingredients to crockpot.
2. Cook on low for 8 hours, or on high for 4 hours.

SOUR CREAM DRIZZLE

SERVES: 4

PER SERVING

CALORIES: 30

FAT: 3G

PROTEIN: 0G

CARBS: 1G

FIBER: 0G

Ingredients:

- 1/4 cup sour cream
- 1/4 tsp chili powder
- 1 TBS water

Directions:

1. Put all of the 'SOUR CREAM DRIZZLE' ingredients in a ziploc bag.

2. Shake it all up to get in mixed well.

3. Cut off a tiny part of the edge (you're making a piping bag out of this)

4. Drizzle as desired

SPAGHETTI & MEATBALLS

SERVES: 4

PER SERVING

CALORIES: 568

FAT: 32G

PROTEIN: 27G

CARBS: 10G

FIBER: 2G

Ingredients:

- 1 lb ground beef
- 2 eggs
- 1/2 tsp onion powder
- 3/4 tsp salt
- 1/2 tsp pepper
- 1/2 tsp garlic powder
- 3/4 cup crushed pork rinds

- 1/4 cup grated parmesan cheese
- 1 tsp Italian seasoning
- 1 tsp parsley
- 2 TBS sugar free ketchup
- 1 1/2 (24oz) jars marinara sauce/ spaghetti sauce (no added sugar) Parmesan cheese, for topping
- Pasta substitute (I love Natural Heaven, Pasta Zero or Spaghetti Squash)

Directions:

1. In a pot, pour tomato sauce, and keep it on a very low simmer.

2. In a mixing bowl, combine ground beef, eggs onion powder, salt, pepper, garlic powder, pork rinds, Parmesan cheese, Italian seasoning, parsley, and sugar free ketchup.

3. Mix well, and form into meatballs.

4. You should make approximately 12.

5. Carefully place them in sauce that's simmering.

6. Cover the pot and let them cook in the sauce for about 20 minutes.

7. Serve over pasta substitute.

SPANISH RICE

SERVES: 4

PER SERVING

CALORIES: 193

FAT: 18G

PROTEIN: 3G

CARBS: 7G

FIBER: 3G

Ingredients:

- 1 bag (12oz.) frozen cauliflower rice (Green Giant)

- 5 TBS butter

- 1/2 tsp garlic powder

- 1/2 tsp onion powder

- 1/4 tsp salt

- 1/2 tsp pepper

- 1/4 cup tomato purée

- Cilantro, optional garnish

Directions:

1. In a skillet, over medium heat, melt butter.

2. Add cauliflower rice, salt, pepper, onion powder, garlic powder.

3. Cook until caulirice is tender, add tomato purée and mix well.

4. Remove from heat and serve.

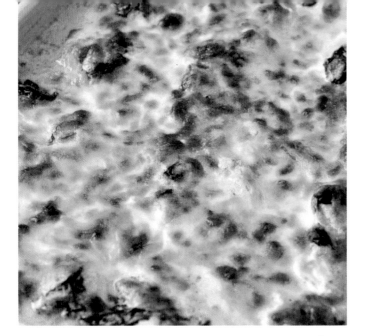

SPINACH DIP CHICKE

SERVES: 6

PER SERVING

CALORIES: 539

FAT: 28G

PROTEIN: 53G

CARBS: 4.5G

FIBER: 1G

Ingredients:

- 3 chicken breasts, cooked & shredded OR 1 rotisserie chicken, shredded
- 1/4 cup bacon, cooked & chopped
- 1/2 tsp parsley
- 1 1/2 tsp Italian seasoning
- 1/4 tsp salt
- 1/4 tsp pepper
- 1/4 tsp garlic powder

- 1/4 tsp onion powder
- 8 oz full fat cream cheese, room temp
- 1 (12 oz) bag frozen spinach, steamed and drained
- 1 cup pepper jack OR mozzarella cheese, shredded FOR TOPPING

Directions:

1. Preheat oven to 350 degrees
2. In a mixing bowl, combine all ingredients (except for mozzarella cheese) well
3. Transfer mixture to 9 inch baking dish and top with shredded cheese.
4. Bake in oven for 10-15 minutes, or until cheese is melted and bubbly.

SUSHI

SERVES: 4

PER SERVING

CALORIES: 230

FAT: 18G

PROTEIN: 22G

CARBS: 7G

FIBER: 4G

Ingredients:

- 6 nori wrappers

- 1 avocado, sliced into wedges

- 4 oz cream cheese, room temp

- 8 oz crabmeat, steamed

- 1/2 lb shrimp, seasoned & cooked

- 1/4-1/2 cup cucumber, sliced into sticks

- Soy sauce, for dipping

- Sriracha mayo

- Sugar free teriyaki sauce, optional topping

- Sesame seeds, topping

Directions:

1. In a food processor, or blender, blend crabmeat and shrimp. Add cream cheese and mix well to combine.

2. Lay nori wrappers out flat, and begin process of assembling rolls

3. Start with approx 2-3 TBS of seafood mixture, add avocado and cucumber.

4. Continue until all wrappers are filled.

5. Carefully, and tightly roll up each filled wrapper and slice.

6. Top with a drizzle of sriracha mayo.

SWEDISH MEATBALL

SERVES: 6

PER SERVING

CALORIES: 400

FAT: 23G

PROTEIN: 19G

CARBS: 4G

FIBER: 1G

Ingredients:

MEATBALLS

- 1 lb ground beef
- 1 lb ground pork
- 1/2 cup onion, finely chopped
- 1/2 tsp salt
- 1/2 tsp pepper
- 1/2 tsp cajun seasoning
- 1/2 tsp garlic powder
- 1/2 tsp onion powder
- 2 eggs
- 1 1/2 TBS parsley

- 1/2 tsp nutmeg
- 1/2 tsp allspice
- 1 TBS Worcestershire sauce
- 1/2 cup crushed pork rinds
- 1/4 cup Parmesan cheese
- ***SAUCE***
- 1 cup beef stock or broth
- 1/2 cup sour cream
- 1/2 cup heavy whipping cream
- 1/4 tsp salt
- 1/4 tsp pepper

Directions:

1. Preheat oven to 350°F

2. In a large mixing bowl, combine all "MEATBALLS" ingredients and roll into balls, and place in 9x13 baking dish.

3. In another bowl, or measuring cup, combine "SAUCE" ingredients.

4. Pour SAUCE ingredients over meatballs and bake in oven for 30-35 minutes.

TACO BAKE

SERVES: 4

PER SERVING

CALORIES: 390

FAT: 27G

PROTEIN: 29G

CARBS: 12.5G

FIBER: 7.5G

Ingredients:

- 1 pound ground beef
- 1 TBS chili powder
- 2 tsp cumin
- 1 tsp pepper
- 1/2 tsp salt
- 2 oz full fat cream cheese

- 1/4 cup water
- 1 cup cheddar cheese, shredded
- 1/2 cup pepper jack cheese, shredded
- 2 low carb tortillas (I use the Mission Low Carb or Great Value Low Carb)
- Garnishes such as lettuce, tomato, sour cream, and avocado are a great addition!

Directions:

1. Preheat oven to 350°F

2. Brown ground beef with seasonings. When it's cooked, add water, cream cheese, and shredded cheese. Mix and combine well.

3. In another bowl, or measuring cup, combine "SAUCE" ingredients.

4. In a baking dish (I use a 10 inch round baking pan) put one low carb tortilla. Add all of the ground meat & cheese mixture, then place the other tortilla on top.

5. Bake in oven for 10 minutes, just to crisp up the tortilla on top. This will add a nice crunch!

TACO CASSEROLE

SERVES: 6

PER SERVING

CALORIES: 575

FAT: 41G

PROTEIN: 42G

CARBS: 6G

FIBER: 2G

Ingredients:

- 2 pounds ground beef
- 1 TBS chili powder
- 1/2 tsp salt
- 1/2 tsp pepper
- 2 tsp cumin
- 1 tsp paprika
- 1/2 tsp onion powder

- 1/4 cup onions, chopped
- 1/4 cup bell pepper (orange, yellow, or red)
- 2 cans Rotel (diced tomatoes with chiles)
- 1 1/2 cup fiesta blend cheese (or similar)
- Optional garnish: sour cream, olives, avocado, guac, jalapeños

Directions:

1. Preheat oven to 350°F
2. In a skillet, cook ground beef, onions, peppers, powdered seasonings, and Rotel.
3. Remove from heat.
4. Transfer to baking dish (9x13 or similar size) and top with shredded cheese.
5. Bake until cheese is bubbly.

TAMALE PIE

SERVES: 6

PER SERVING

CALORIES: 545

FAT: 42G

PROTEIN: 31G

CARBS: 10G

FIBER: 3G

Ingredients:

"Cornbread" Ingredients

- 1 cup almond flour
- 1 tsp baking powder
- 2 eggs
- 1/2 cup cheddar cheese
- 2 TBS heavy whipping cream
- 1/2 cup sour cream
- 4 TBS butter, melted OR oil
- 1 TBS sweetener
- OPTIONAL ADD-IN: jalapeños

"Filling" Ingredients

- 1/2 cup enchilada sauce
- 1 (7 oz) can diced green chiles, drained
- 2 lbs ground beef
- 2 TBS chili powder
- 2 tsp cumin
- 1 tsp paprika
- 1 tsp onion powder
- 1 cup shredded cheddar cheese

Optional Toppings

Sour cream, green onions, avocado, jalapeños

Directions:

1. Preheat oven to 350°F

2. In a mixing bowl, combine all "Cornbread" ingredients. Set aside.

3. In a skillet, cook ground beef and season with powdered seasonings listed.

4. Remove from heat and mix in green chiles, enchilada sauce and cheddar cheese.

5. Spray 9 inch baking dish with nonstick spray.

6. Add "Filling" ingredients

7. Layer "Cornbread" batter on top

8. Bake in oven for 30-40 minutes, or until Cornbread is golden top.

9. Let it rest for 15 minutes, or so, to set up.

THAI PEANUT CHICKE

SERVES: 4

PER SERVING

CALORIES: 492

FAT: 25G

PROTEIN: 37G

CARBS: 7G

FIBER: 3G

Ingredients:

CHICKEN:

- 6 boneless skinless chicken thighs

- 1/4 tsp pepper

- 1/4 tsp garlic powder

- 1 tsp sesame seeds

- 1 TBS soy sauce or coconut aminos

- 2 TBS oil (avocado or olive oil)

- 1 tsp ginger (minced or paste)

- 1 tsp sweetener (erythritol or stevia)

PEANUT SAUCE:

- 1/2 cup peanut butter or nut butter, sugar free/ unsweetened

- 1/2 TBS soy sauce or coconut aminos

- 1 tsp minced garlic

- 1/2 tsp ginger (mincers or paste)

- 2 TBS water

- 2 TBS sweetener (erythritol or stevia)

Garnishes:

- Lettuce (For presentation purposes, you'll make a bed of lettuce)

- Green onion

- Sesame seeds

Directions:

1. In a skillet, heat oil, and add all "Chicken Ingredients" cook thoroughly.

2. Remove from heat.

3. Combine all "Peanut Sauce Ingredients" in a blender and mix it up for a few seconds.

4. Serve on a bed of lettuce, and garnish with green onion and sesame seeds.

TOSTADAS

SERVES: 4

PER SERVING

CALORIES: 432

FAT: 33G

PROTEIN: 28G

CARBS: 4G

FIBER: 2G

Ingredients:

TACO MEAT INGREDIENTS:

- 1 pound ground beef
- 1 1/2 TBS chili powder
- 1 tsp cumin
- 1 tsp paprika
- 1/2 tsp onion powder
- 1/2 tsp salt
- 1/2 tsp pepper

Tostada shells:

- 1 cup shredded cheddar cheese

Toppings:

- Lettuce, tomato guac, olives, sour cream drizzle (see SOUR CREAM DRIZZLE recipe)

Directions:

1. Brown ground beef in skillet with seasonings.

2. While that's cooking, make tostada shells.

3. To make shells, spread a circle (about 1/4 cup) of shredded cheese on parchment paper and microwave for 90 seconds.

4. Immediately remove from microwave and let it firm up while laying flat. The cheese should be the color of a Dorito (lol).

5. Top shells with meat and toppings, and enjoy!

TUSCAN CHICKEN

SERVES: 6

PER SERVING

CALORIES: 365

FAT: 25G

PROTEIN: 30G

CARBS: 4G

FIBER: 1G

Ingredients:

- 1 1/2 lbs boneless skinless chicken breasts, sliced thin

- 2 TBS avocado oil

- 1 cup heavy whipping cream

- 1/2 cup chicken broth

- 1/2 tsp salt

- 1/2 tsp pepper

- 1/2 tsp garlic powder

- 1/4 tsp onion powder

- 1 tsp Italian seasoning

- 1/2 cup Parmesan cheese

- 1 (12 oz) bag frozen spinach, steamed & drained

- 1/4 cup grape tomatoes, sliced in half

Directions:

1. In a skillet, over medium heat, add oil and chicken, tomatoes and powdered seasonings.

2. Cook for 3-5 minutes on each side, or until it's no longer pink in the middle.

3. Remove from skillet, and set aside.

4. In the same skillet, add cream, broth, and spinach.

5. Cook over low heat until sauce begins to thicken.

6. Add chicken back to pan with sauce.

VEGGIE & SAUSAGE CASSEROLE

SERVES: 8

PER SERVING

CALORIES: 430

FAT: 40G

PROTEIN: 17G

CARBS: 9G

FIBER: 2G

Ingredients:

- 1 (12 oz) bag broccoli florets, steamed & drained
- 1 (12 oz) bag cauliflower, steamed & drained
- 2 TBS avocado oil
- 1/2 cup onion, chopped
- 2 TBS minced garlic
- 1 pack (14 oz) smoked sausage, sliced

- 8 oz cream cheese, cubed
- 1/4 cup mayo
- 2 cups shredded cheddar cheese
- 1/4 tsp salt
- 1/2 tsp pepper
- 1/4 tsp cajun seasoning

Directions:

1. Preheat oven to 375°F

2. In a skillet, over medium heat, add oil, onions and sausage. Sauté until onions are tender and sausage is slightly crispy. Remove from heat.

3. In a 9x13 baking dish, combine all ingredients and stir well.

4. Bake for 15 - 20 minutes, or until everything is melted and to is golden.

WEDGE SALAD

SERVES: 4

PER SERVING

CALORIES: 361

FAT: 32G

PROTEIN: 13G

CARBS: 4G

FIBER: 2G

Ingredients:

- 1 head iceberg lettuce
- 4 slices bacon, cooked & crumbled
- 1 cup grape tomatoes, diced
- 2 stalks green onion, chopped
- Dressing Options
  - Blue Cheese Dressing
  - Ranch Dressing

Directions:

1. Remove the outer leaves of the head of lettuce and the core.

2. If you hit the core of the head of lettuce on the counter, it will break it lose and you can pull it right out.

3. Cut the head of lettuce into quarters, and rinse with water. Set on a towel to let the water drain out.

4. Plate the wedges and top with dressing, bacon, tomatoes, and green onion.

ZUPPA TOSCANA SOUP

SERVES: 6

PER SERVING

CALORIES: 310

FAT: 20G

PROTEIN: 25G

CARBS: 8G

FIBER: 2G

Ingredients:

- 2 (16 oz) packs Italian sausage
- 6 strips bacon, raw & chopped
- 1/2 cup onion, chopped
- 3 TBS minced garlic
- 6 cups chicken broth or stock
- 1/2 cup celery, finely chopped
- 4 cups spinach, fresh

- 1 cup heavy whipping cream
- 4 TBS parmesan cheese
- 1/2 tsp salt
- 1 tsp pepper
- 1/4 tsp cajun seasoning
- 1 tsp parsley

Directions:

1. In a large pot, over medium heat, add onions and sausage.

2. Cook sausage about halfway, then add bacon pieces.

3. When the onions are tender and the meat is cooked, reduce heat to low and add all remaining ingredients.

4. Simmer for just a few minutes until it's heated all the way through.

5. Remove from heat and serve.

Made in the USA
Coppell, TX
22 May 2021